S0-BDA-565

Houghton
Mifflin
Harcourt

Math
Expressions

Volume 1

Dr. Karen C. Fuson
and
Dr. Sybilla Beckmann

This material is based upon work supported by the
National Science Foundation
under Grant Numbers
ESI-9816320, REC-9806020, and RED-935373.

Any opinions, findings, and conclusions, or recommendations expressed in this material
are those of the author and do not necessarily reflect the views of the National Science Foundation.

Teacher Reviewers

Kindergarten
Patricia Stroh Sugiyama
Wilmette, Illinois

Barbara Wahle
Evanston, Illinois

Grade 1
Sandra Budson
Newton, Massachusetts

Janet Pecci
Chicago, Illinois

Megan Rees
Chicago, Illinois

Grade 2
Molly Dunn
Danvers, Massachusetts

Agnes Lesnick
Hillside, Illinois

Rita Soto
Chicago, Illinois

Grade 3
Jane Curran
Honesdale, Pennsylvania

Sandra Tucker
Chicago, Illinois

Grade 4
Sara Stoneberg Llibre
Chicago, Illinois

Sheri Roedel
Chicago, Illinois

Grade 5
Todd Atler
Chicago, Illinois

Leah Barry
Norfolk, Massachusetts

Grade 6
Jean S. Armstrong
Austin, Texas

Cheryl Van Ness
Dunellen, New Jersey

VOLUME 1 CONTENTS

* This lesson consists only of activities from the Teacher Edition.

Dear Family,

Your child is learning math in an innovative program called *Math Expressions*. The program emphasizes understanding and fluency. Your child will

- connect math to daily life.

- solve a problem by understanding and representing the situation and then finding the solution.

- work with and explain strategies to other students.

Visualizing and talking about math is very important. This approach helps children feel that they can learn math. They do learn math, enjoy doing so, and feel good about themselves as math learners.

Recent research shows that effort is important in getting smarter and in doing well in math. This is called effort-produced ability. Students who work hard, think and participate in class, and do their homework do learn math. So encourage your child to work hard and to know that he or she can learn math.

Your child will have math homework almost every day. Homework is important for math learning. Make a special time for homework in a quiet place. Ask your child to explain to you some problem he or she did.

To make concepts clearer, the *Math Expressions* program uses some special methods and visual supports. Some of these for Unit 1 are shown on the back. More information for families is on the Web at http://www.thinkcentral.com/.

If your child has problems with math, please send me a note or talk to me to see how we can work together to help your child.

Thank you. You are vital to your child's learning.

continued ▶

In our math class, we are exploring the ideas of rate, ratio, and proportion.

A rate tells how much is used repeatedly in a given situation. For example, $8 *per package* means $8 *for each package* or $8 *for every package*.

The ratio of one number to another is a simple way to express the relative size of two quantities or measurements.

A proportion is an equation that shows two equivalent ratios. It can be written 6:14 = 15:35   or   6:14 :: 15:35.

In a proportion problem, one of the four numbers is unknown. For example:

> Grandma made applesauce using the same number of bags of red apples and bags of yellow apples. Her red apples cost $6 and her yellow apples cost $14. I used her recipe but made more applesauce. I paid $35 for my yellow apples. How much did my red apples cost?

The problem makes this proportion:

$$6:14 = c:35$$

To solve this proportion, we can put the ratios in a Factor Puzzle.

$$c \text{ is } 3 \times 5 = 15$$

The Factor Puzzle is from the rows of the ratio table that are × 2 (• 2) and × 5 (• 5) of the basic ratio 3:7. Factor Puzzles enable your child to understand and solve challenging proportion problems.

Discuss with your child how you use proportions in your life, such as when you double a recipe.

If you have any questions, please call or write to me.

Sincerely,
Your child's teacher

Factor Puzzle

Red Yellow

	3	7	
2	6	14	2
5	15	35	5
	3	7	

Ratio Table

	R	Y
Bags	3	:	7
1	3 : 7
2	6 : 14
3	9 : 21
4	12 : 28
5	15 : 35
6	18 : 42
7	21 : 49
8	24 : 56
9	27 : 63

• 2 (next to row 2)
• 5 (next to row 5)

COMMON CORE

This unit includes the Common Core Standards for Mathematical Content for Ratios and Proportional Relationships, 6.RP.1, 6.RP.2, 6.RP.3, 6.RP.3a, 6.RP.3b; Expressions and Equations, 6.EE.6, 6.EE.9; The Number System, 6.NS.4 and all Mathematical Practices.

Factor Puzzles and the Multiplication Table

Carta a la familia

Estimada familia,

Su hijo está aprendiendo matemáticas mediante un innovador programa llamado *Expresiones en matemáticas*. Este programa enfatiza la comprensión y el dominio de los conocimientos. Con este programa, su hijo aprenderá a:

- relacionar las matemáticas con la vida diaria.

- resolver problemas mediante la comprensión y la representación de diferentes situaciones.

- trabajar con diferentes estrategias y a explicarlas a otros estudiantes.

La visualización y las charlas matemáticas son muy importantes. Cuando se usan, facilitan el aprendizaje. Mediante ellas el alumno aprende, disfruta mientras lo hace, y adquiere una buena autoestima como estudiante de matemáticas.

Estudios recientes han demostrado que esforzarse es muy importante para el desarrollo de la inteligencia y el estudio de las matemáticas. A este proceso se le llama adquisición de destrezas mediante esfuerzo. Para aprender, los estudiantes deben trabajar, concentrarse y participar durante la clase, y realizar tareas en la casa. Por esto, le pedimos que anime a su hijo a completar sus trabajos.

Casi diariamente su hijo tendrá tarea para la casa. La tarea es una parte muy importante del aprendizaje de las matemáticas. Para realizarla, designe un tiempo especial en un lugar tranquilo. Al terminar, pida a su hijo que le explique cómo resolvió algunos de los problemas.

Para lograr que los conceptos sean más claros, el programa *Expresiones en matemáticas* utiliza algunos métodos especiales y refuerzos visuales. Algunos de los que corresponden a la Unidad 1 se muestran en la parte de atrás. Puede hallar más información para la familia en Internet en http://www.thinkcentral.com/.

Si su hijo tiene problemas en la asignatura de matemáticas, por favor comuníquese conmigo para que unidos hallemos la mejor manera de ayudarlo.

Gracias. Usted es imprescindible para el aprendizaje de su hijo.

continúa ▶

En nuestra clase de matemáticas, estamos estudiando los conceptos de tasa, razón y proporción.

Una tasa indica cuánto se usa algo repetidamente en una situación dada. Por ejemplo, $8 *por paquete* significa $8 *por cada paquete*.

La razón de un número a otro es una manera simple de expresar el tamaño relativo de dos cantidades o medidas.

Una proporción es una ecuación que muestra dos razones equivalentes. Puede escribirse así:

6:14 = 15:35   o   6:14 :: 15:35.

En un problema de proporción, uno de los cuatro números es un número desconocido. Por ejemplo:

Para hacer puré de manzanas, mi abuelita usó el mismo número de bolsas de manzanas rojas que de manzanas amarillas. Las bolsas de manzanas rojas costaron $6 y las de amarillas $14. Yo usé la misma receta, pero hice más puré. Si pagué $35 por mis manzanas amarillas, ¿cuánto pagué por las rojas?

Rompecabezas de factores

Rojo Amarillo

	3	7	
2	6	14	2
5	15	35	5
	3	7	

El problema se representa con esta proporción:

6:14 = c:35

Para resolver esta proporción, podemos hacer un rompecabezas de factores con las razones.

c es 3 × 5 = 15

El rompecabezas de factores se hace con las hileras de la tablas de razones que son × 2 (• 2) y × 5 (• 5) de la razón básica 3:7. Los rompecabezas de factores sirven para resolver problemas difíciles de proporciones.

Comente con su hijo acerca de situaciones de su vida diaria en las que se usen proporciones, tal como hacer el doble de alguna receta de cocina.

Si tiene cualquier pregunta, por favor comuníquese conmigo.

Atentamente,

El maestro de su hijo.

Tabla de razones

Bolsas	R	A
	3	7
1	3	7
• 2 → 2	6	14
3	9	21
4	12	28
• 5 → 5	15	35
6	18	42
7	21	49
8	24	56
9	27	63

COMMON CORE

Esta unidad incluye los Common Core Standards for Mathematical Content for Ratios and Proportional Relationships, 6.RP.1, 6.RP.2, 6.RP.3, 6.RP.3a, 6.RP.3b; Expressions and Equations, 6.EE.6, 6.EE.9; The Number System, 6.NS.4 and all Mathematical Practices.

Name _____ Date _____

▶ Discuss Patterns in the Multiplication Table

Look for patterns in the multiplication tables.

Table 1

•	1	2	3	4	5	6	7	8	9
1	1	2	3	4	5	6	7	8	9
2	2	4	6	8	10	12	14	16	18
3	3	6	9	12	15	18	21	24	27
4	4	8	12	16	20	24	28	32	36
5	5	10	15	20	25	30	35	40	45
6	6	12	18	24	30	36	42	48	54
7	7	14	21	28	35	42	49	56	63
8	8	16	24	32	40	48	56	64	72
9	9	18	27	36	45	54	63	72	81

Table 2

•	1	2	3	4	5	6	7	8	9
1	1	2	3	4	5	6	7	8	9
2	2	4	6	8	10	12	14	16	18
3	3	6	9	12	15	18	21	24	27
4	4	8	12	16	20	24	28	32	36
5	5	10	15	20	25	30	35	40	45
6	6	12	18	24	30	36	42	48	54
7	7	14	21	28	35	42	49	56	63
8	8	16	24	32	40	48	56	64	72
9	9	18	27	36	45	54	63	72	81

▶ Strategies for Finding Factors

Write the missing **factors** and the missing **product**.

1. **Table 3**

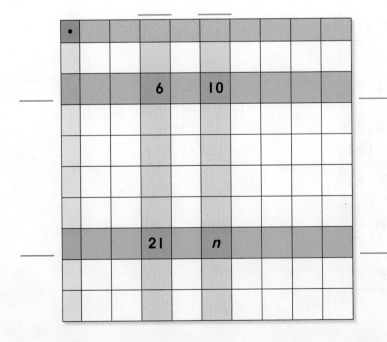

Factor Puzzle

6	10
21	

Name _____   Date _____

▶ Solve Factor Puzzles

Write the missing factors and the missing product.

2. Table 4

•								
	6				21			
	16				n			

Factor Puzzle

6	21
16	

3. Table 5

•	2	4	7	1	5	3	6	8	9
3	6	12	21	3	15	9	18	24	27
1	2	4	7	1	5	3	6	8	9
4	8	16	28	4	20	12	24	32	36
2	4	8	14	2	10	6	12	16	18
7	14	28	49	7	35	21	42	56	63
9	18	36	63	9	45	27	54	72	81
5	10	20	35	5	25	15	30	40	45
8	16	32	56	8	40	24	48	64	72
6	12	24	42	6	30	18	36	48	54

Factor Puzzle

	6
35	15

Factor Puzzles and the Multiplication Table

▶ Practice with Factor Puzzles

Solve each Factor Puzzle.

1.

20	15
8	

2.

8	14
	21

3.

	28
24	32

4.

24	
32	36

5.

20	35
	56

6.

	16
35	56

7.

21	24
28	

8.

	10
63	18

9.

35	
15	24

10.

24	28
54	

11.

56	63
	81

12.

54	63
24	

13.

36	63
8	

14.

32	36
	63

15.

	54
56	48

UNIT 1 LESSON 2

Solving Factor Puzzles **7**

Name _____

Date _____

▶ Make Factor Puzzles

Make your own Factor Puzzles. Exchange with a classmate.

16.

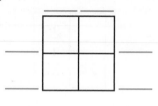

17.

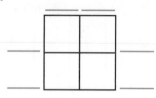

18.

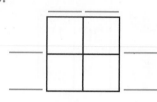

19.

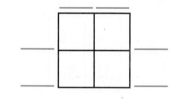

20.

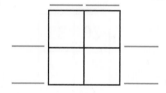

21.

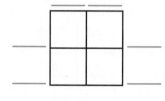

22.

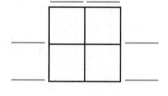

23.

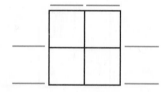

24.

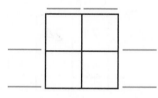

25.

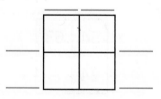

26.

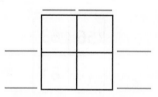

27.

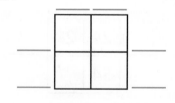

28.

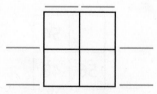

29.

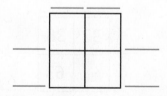

30.

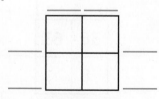

► Find the Total So Far

Noreen started to save money. Every day she put three $1 coins into her duck bank. Write how much money she had each day.

Noreen begins with an empty bank.		Noreen begins with $0 in her bank.
1. On Day 1 Noreen put $3 into her bank.		On Day 1 Noreen had $ _____ in her bank.
2. On Day 2 Noreen put $3 into her bank.		On Day 2 Noreen had $ _____ in her bank.
3. On Day 3 Noreen put $3 into her bank.		On Day 3 Noreen had $ _____ in her bank.
4. On Day 4 Noreen put $3 into her bank.		On Day 4 Noreen had $ _____ in her bank.
5. On Day 5 Noreen put $3 into her bank.		On Day 5 Noreen had $ _____ in her bank.
6. On Day 6 Noreen put $3 into her bank.		On Day 6 Noreen had $ _____ in her bank.

Noreen continues to put $3 into her bank every day.

7. On Day 10, Noreen had _____ in her bank.

8. On Day 12, Noreen had _____ in her bank.

Name _____   **Date** _____

Vocabulary
rate table

▶ Complete a Rate Table

This **rate table** shows Noreen's savings.

9. Fill in the rest of the table to show how much money Noreen saved each day and how much her total was each day.

Days	Dollars
1	3
2	6
3	

} + 3

10. What did you write between each row? _____

11. What does the number between each row show?

_____

_____

▶ Identify Rate Tables

These tables show four different ways Noreen could have saved money. Complete each table. Then decide which tables are rate tables and which are not. Explain why.

12.

Days	Dollars
1	2
2	
3	
4	
5	
6	

} + 2
} + 2
} + 2
} + 2
} + 2

_____

_____

_____

_____

_____

Rate Situations and Rate Tables

▶ Identify Rate Tables (continued)

13.

Days	Dollars
1	4
2	12
3	18
4	20
5	24
6	28

14.

Days	Dollars
1	7
2	14
3	21
4	28
5	35
6	42

15.

Days	Dollars
1	3
2	5
3	5
4	9
5	11
6	14

Name _____   **Date** _____

▶ Practice Factor Puzzles

Solve each Factor Puzzle.

16.

	32
27	72

17.

10	12
	54

18.

	24
21	28

19.

8	
12	27

20.

24	30
28	

21.

	12
10	8

22.

56	24
35	

23.

	24
28	21

24.

16	56
	21

Make your own Factor Puzzles. Exchange with a classmate.

25.

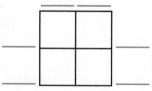

26.

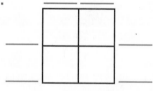

27.

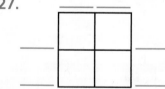

28.

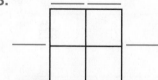

29.

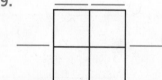

30.

Rate Situations and Rate Tables

▶ Rates and Multiplication

Vocabulary

unit rate
constant rate
every
each
per

1. Pedro and Pilar collect snails. Each day they add 4 snails to their tank. How many snails do they have after 5 days?

   _____

2. We can make a rate table to find the answer for any number of days. Fill in the rest of the rate table. Write the multiplications to the left of the table.

3. Where in the rate table is the answer to Problem 1 and why is it there?

   _____

   _____

   _____

   _____

Unit   Product

Days	Snails
1	4
2	8
3	
4	
5	

+4

▶ Equal-Groups Multiplication and Rates

A rate problem can be thought of as an equal-groups multiplication.
The multiplier is a unit that counts the number of groups.
The **unit rate** is the amount in 1 group.

number of equal groups	•	amount in 1 group	=	total
multiplier	•	unit rate	=	product
number of days	•	4 snails each day	=	total number of snails so far

If the same rate is repeated, the rate is a **constant rate**.
Look for special words that show a constant rate.

The rate is 4 snails **every** day.

The rate is 4 snails **each** day.

The rate is 4 snails **per** day.

▶ Identify Rate Situations

For each situation, decide whether there is a constant rate.
If *yes*, write the rate and complete the rate table.

4. In the zoo, 7 kangaroos live in each kangaroo house.

   Is there a constant rate? _____

   _____ _____ per _____ .

Unit	Product
___	___
1	
2	
3	

5. In the last 3 weeks, Ben saw 3 films, then 4 films, and then 3 films.

   Is there a constant rate? _____

   _____ _____ per _____ .

Unit	Product
___	___
1	
2	
3	

6. Tara made 9 drawings on each page of her sketchbook.

   Is there a constant rate? _____

   _____ _____ per _____ .

Unit	Product
___	___
1	
2	
3	

7. A bagging machine puts 3 oranges, then 5 oranges, and then 4 oranges in a bag.

   Is there a constant rate? _____

   _____ _____ per _____ .

Unit	Product
___	___
1	
2	
3	

8. There are 7 days in every week.

   Is there a constant rate? _____

   _____ _____ per _____ .

Unit	Product
___	___
1	
2	
3	

9. A bagging machine always puts 5 oranges in a bag.

   Is there a constant rate? _____

   _____ _____ per _____ .

Unit	Product
___	___
1	
2	
3	

Rate Situations and Unit Rate Language

▶ Is a Constant Rate Reasonable?

For each rate situation, fill in the rate information and the rate table. Label the columns in the table.

Discuss what you assume in order for the situation to be a rate situation in the real world.

1. Every day of this week Joanne made 3 of her free throws.

_____ _____ per _____ .

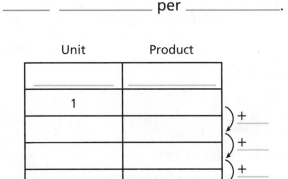

Unit	Product
_____	_____
1	

2. Efrain makes 8 sketches on each page of his drawing book.

_____ _____ per _____ .

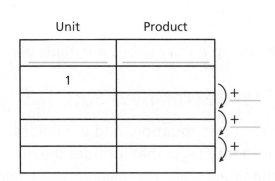

Unit	Product
_____	_____
1	

3. Abby uses 2 cups of flour in each loaf of bread she makes.

_____ _____ per _____ .

Unit	Product
_____	_____
1	

4. Eusebio planted 7 tomato vines in each yard he takes care of.

_____ _____ per _____ .

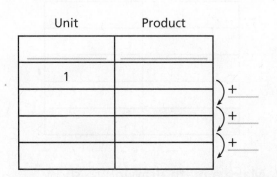

Unit	Product
_____	_____
1	

Name _____   Date _____

Vocabulary

scrambled rate table

▶ Is It a Rate Table?

Decide whether each table is a rate table. Explain why or why not.

5. _____ _____

1	9
2	18
3	27
4	36
5	45

6. _____ _____

1	4
2	5
3	9
4	10
5	14

7. _____ _____

1	11
2	22
3	33
4	44
5	55

8. _____ _____

1	3
2	5
3	8
4	10
5	13

_____   _____   _____   _____

_____   _____   _____   _____

9. Make up a story about one table and label the table.

▶ Make Scrambled Rate Tables and Math Drawings

For each rate situation, find the unit rate and write it using *per*.
Make a rate table that includes the given information as the first row
in the table. Continue making a **scrambled rate table**.

10. The store sold 5 sacks of oranges
    for $30.

_____ _____ per _____.

Unit	Product

11. Grandpa's rectangular garden has
    24 pepper plants in the first 4 rows.

_____ _____ per _____.

Unit	Product

12. Make a math drawing to show
    the first row of your rate table
    for Exercise 10.

13. Make a math drawing to show
    the first row of your rate table
    for Exercise 11.

Unit Rates, Products and Rate Tables

Name _____ Date _____

▶ Unit Pricing Situations

These three rate tables show the prices of three different kinds of granola. Each has a different **unit price**. Fill in the missing values in each table.

Table 1

1.

Number of Pounds	Cost in Dollars
1	3
2	
3	
	12
5	
6	
	21

Table 2

2.

Number of Pounds	Cost in Dollars
1	6
2	
3	
	24
	30
10	
	600

Table 3

3.

Number of Pounds	Cost in Dollars
1	
8	
	10
6	30
	100
	20
5	

▶ What's the Error?

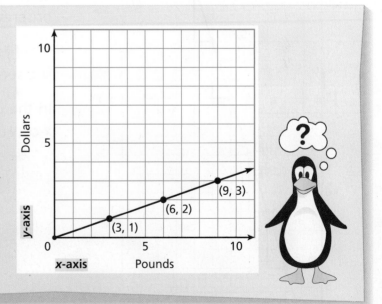

Dear Math Students,

I made this graph to show the first three rows from Table 1. When I tried to draw the **unit rate triangle**, I realized that I did something wrong.

Can you help me figure out what mistake I made?

Your friend,
Puzzled Penguin

4. Write a response to Puzzled Penguin. Then draw the correct graph in the **coordinate plane** above.

_____

_____

Name _____   Date _____

Vocabulary

ordered pair
x-coordinate
y-coordinate

▶ Relate Table, Equation, and Graph

Number of Pounds	Cost in Dollars
1	3
2	6
3	9
4	12
5	15
6	18
7	21

Number of Pounds	•	Unit Rate	=	Cost in Dollars
p	•	*r*	=	*C*
1	•	3	=	3
2	•	3	=	6
3	•	3	=	9
4	•	3	=	12
5	•	3	=	15
6	•	3	=	18
7	•	3	=	21

Number of Pounds	Cost in Dollars	
1	• 3	③
2	• 3	6
3	• 3	9
4	• 3	12
5	• 3	15
6	• 3	18
7	• 3	21

The unit rate is circled. Imagine the unit rate written on the vertical rule to be multiplied by the number in the left column to get the number in the right column.

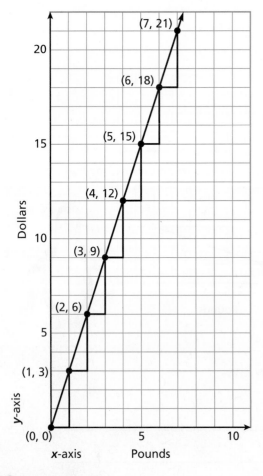

Each point on the graph corresponds to an **ordered pair**. (0, 0) and (1, 3) are ordered pairs.

The first number is the ***x*-coordinate** and the second number is the ***y*-coordinate**.

In the ordered pair (1, 3), 1 is the *x*-coordinate and 3 is the *y*-coordinate.

Unit Pricing

Name _____   Date _____

▶ Constant Speed Situations

1. Dan ran in the Grade 6 track meet.

	Time	Distance
	Seconds	**Yards**
	1	
	3	15
	9	
		10
	50	

a. Unit rate: ___ _____ per _____

b. What are the sides of the unit rate triangle for the graph?

c. Draw the graph.

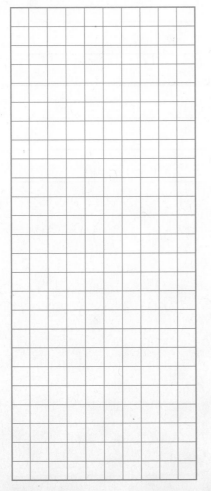

2. Julie rode her bike in the bike festival.

	Time	Distance
	Hours	**Miles**
	1	
	2	
	4	44
		33

a. Unit rate: ___ _____ per _____

b. What are the sides of the unit rate triangle for the graph?

c. Draw the graph.

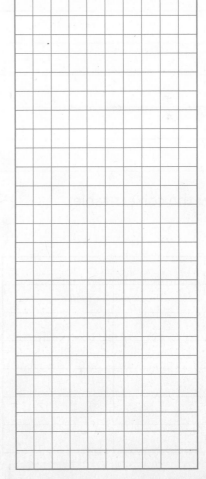

▶ What's the Error?

Dear Math Students,

My friend Gavin also ran in the Grade 6 track meet. His unit rate was 4 yards per second. I made this table of Gavin's times and distances. Gavin says that my table is not correct. Can you help me?

Your friend,
Puzzled Penguin

Time	Distance
Seconds	Yards
4	1
8	2
12	3
16	4
32	8
36	9

3. Write a response to Puzzled Penguin.

_____

_____

_____

_____

_____

_____

4. Show the correct table.

▶ Review of Rate Situations

5. Use the graph to fill in the rows of the rate table.
   Circle the unit rate in the table. Draw the unit rate triangle in the graph.

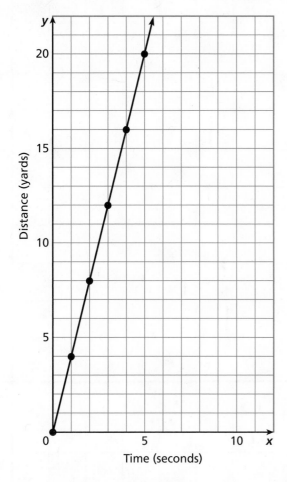

Time	Distance
Seconds	Yards
3	
1	
	8
5	
	16

Solve each rate problem.

6. Ron earns $5 per hour for raking leaves. How much will he earn in 6 hours?

   _____

7. Mr. Martin drives at a constant rate of 50 miles per hour for 3 hours. How far does he drive?

   _____

8. Margo buys 4 pounds of peaches for $12. What is the unit rate?

   _____

9. Karen walks 6 miles in 2 hours. What is her unit rate?

   _____

 10. **On the Back** Make a rate table for 1 to 5 pounds and draw a graph for the situation in Problem 8.

Constant Speed

Name _____   **Date** _____

Vocabulary

Linked Rate Table
ratio table

▶ Ratio Tables as Linked Rate Tables

Noreen saves $3 a day and Tim saves $5 a day. They start saving
on the same day. The **Linked Rate Table** and the **ratio table**
show Noreen's and Tim's savings.

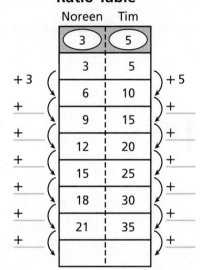

Linked Rate Table

Days	Noreen ③	Tim ⑤
1	3	5
2	6	10
3	9	15
4	12	20
5	15	25
6	18	30
7	21	35

Ratio Table

Noreen ③	Tim ⑤
3	5
6	10
9	15
12	20
15	25
18	30
21	35

1. How are the tables alike? How are they different?

_____

_____

_____

2. What are the numbers circled at the top of each table? _____

3. Fill in the numbers to the left and right of the ratio table to show
   Noreen's and Tim's constant increases.

Use the tables to answer each question.

4. Noreen has saved $12.

   How much has Tim saved? _____

   On which day was this? _____

5. Tim has saved $35.

   How much has Noreen saved? _____

   On which day was this? _____

6. On what day will Noreen have $30 in her bank? _____

   Why? _____

   How much will Tim have then? _____

▶ Relate Drawings and Ratio Tables

Discuss relationships you see.

• How is the ratio table related to the multiplication table?

• How is the ratio table related to two rate tables?

• How are the constant increases shown in the drawing and in the ratio table?

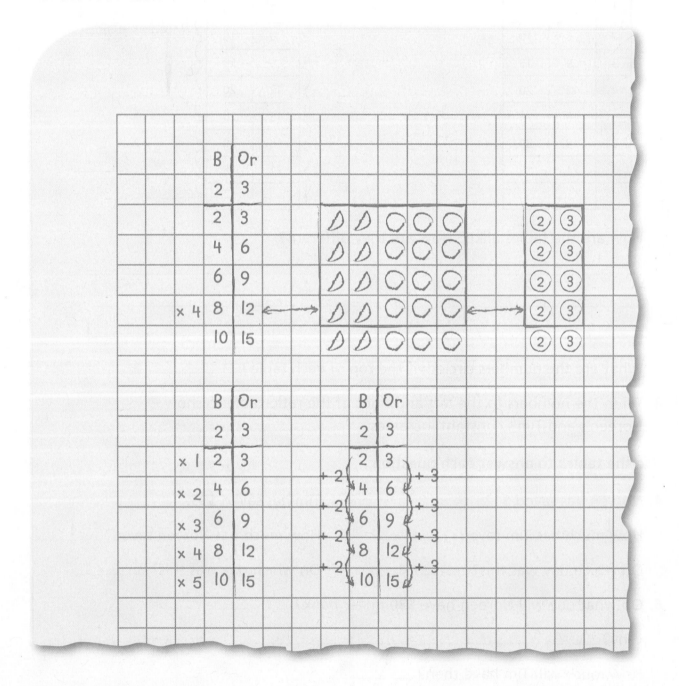

▶ Make a Ratio Table

Make a ratio table for each situation. Be sure to label the columns.

1. Noreen makes 2 drawings on each page of her sketchbook. Tim makes 5 drawings on each page of his sketchbook.

2. Two bands march onto the football field. Band 1 marches on in rows of 5 and Band 2 marches on in rows of 7.

3. John can plant 7 tomato vines in the time it takes Joanna to plant 4 tomato vines.

Ratio Table 1

+ ___ + ___
+ ___ + ___
+ ___ + ___
+ ___ + ___
+ ___ + ___

The linking unit is

_____.

Ratio Table 2

Rows

The linking unit is

_____.

Ratio Table 3

The linking unit is

_____.

▶ Ratio Language and Symbols

4. The ratio of Noreen's drawings to Tim's drawings is _____ to _____.

5. a. The ratio of the people in Band 1 to the people in Band 2 is _____ to

   _____ written as 5:7.

   b. If Band 1 has 15 people on the field, Band 2 has _____ people on

   the field. This is _____ rows.

6. a. John and Joanna's tomato vines are in the ratio of _____ to _____.

   b. We write this as _____ : _____.

   c. If John plants 42 tomato vines, Joanna plants _____.

   d. If Joanna plants 8 tomato vines, John plants _____.

Name _____

Date _____

Vocabulary

basic ratio
equivalent ratios

▶ Recognize Ratio and Non-Ratio Tables

7. Discuss which are ratio tables and why. Tell ratio stories
   for each ratio table and tell what the linking unit and
   the column labels are for each story.

A.

4	7
8	14
12	21
16	28
20	35
24	42
28	49
32	56

B.

3	5
6	12
9	18
12	20
15	24
18	30
21	33
24	42

C.

2	9
4	18
6	27
8	36
10	45
12	54
14	63
16	72

D.

2	3
5	6
7	9
11	12
13	15
16	18
20	21
22	24

▶ Basic Ratios and Equivalent Ratios

A **basic ratio** has the least possible whole numbers.
4:7 is a basic ratio because no whole number (except 1)
divides evenly into 4 and 7.

Equivalent ratios are made up of multiples of the basic ratio row.
Equivalent ratios are written as 8:14 = 20:35 or 8:14 :: 20:35.

8. For the tables that are ratio tables, use the tables to write four pairs of
   equivalent ratios.

A. _____   _____

   _____   _____

B. _____   _____

   _____   _____

C. _____   _____

   _____   _____

D. _____   _____

   _____   _____

▶ Proportions and Factor Puzzles

Two equivalent ratios make a **proportion**.
Any two rows from a ratio table make a proportion.
In a proportion problem, one of the four numbers is unknown.
Solving a proportion means finding that unknown number.

Proportion problem:

Grandma made applesauce using the same number of bags
of red apples and bags of yellow apples. Her red apples cost $6
and her yellow apples cost $14. I used her recipe but made
more applesauce. I paid $35 for my yellow apples. How much
did my red apples cost?

The problem can be solved by solving this proportion:

$$6{:}14 = c{:}35$$

To solve the proportion, you need to find the value of c.

1. Fill in the ratio table for the problem.

2. Circle the rows of the ratio table that make up the problem.

3. a. What is the value of c? _____

   b. What is the solution to the problem? _____

Ratio Table

Bags	R	Y
	◯	: ◯
1		:
2		:
3		:
4		:
5		:
6		:
7		:
8		:
9		:

You know how to solve Factor Puzzles. It is faster to make a
Factor Puzzle than a whole ratio table.

4. Write the numbers from the proportion problem in the Factor
   Puzzle. Solve the Factor Puzzle.

5. Where in the ratio table are the numbers above and below
   the Factor Puzzle? _____

6. Where in the ratio table are the numbers to the left and
   right of the Factor Puzzle? _____

   Write these two numbers with a multiplication sign to the left
   of the yellow column in the ratio table.

7. Where in the ratio table is your answer? _____

Factor Puzzle

Red Yellow

6	14
	35

▶ Solve Proportion Problems

Use Factor Puzzles to solve these proportion problems. Noreen and Tim both do these activities for the same amount of time but at their own constant rates.

Ratio Table

N   T

○ : ○

:

:

:

:

:

:

:

:

:

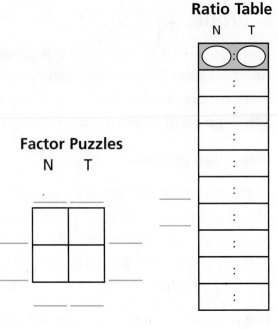

Factor Puzzles

N   T

8. a. Noreen saved $20 while Tim saved $35. When Noreen has saved $24, how much will Tim have saved?

_____

b. Fill in the ratio table. Circle the rows that make the Factor Puzzle and write the multipliers for those rows outside the table.

N   T

9. While Noreen plants 6 tomato plants, Tim plants 10 tomato plants. When Noreen has planted 21 tomato plants, how many will Tim have planted?

_____ plants

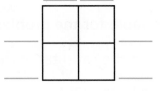

N   T

10. When Noreen had collected 6 stickers, Tim had collected 21 stickers. How many stickers will Noreen have when Tim has 56 stickers?

_____ stickers

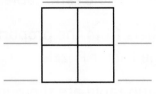

11. Noreen did 72 push-ups while Tim did 32 push-ups. When Tim had done 12 push-ups, how many had Noreen done?

_____ push-ups

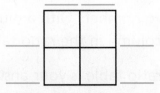

Name _____   Date _____

▶ Make Assumptions

Write the assumptions that must be stated to make the problem a proportion problem. Make and label a Factor Puzzle for the problem. Box the unknown and solve the puzzle and the problem.

1. Two bands march in rows onto the football field. When Band A has 15 people on the field, Band B has 6. When Band B has 14 people on the field, how many people will Band A have on the field?

   _____ _____ _____   _____

   _____

   _____

   Problem solution: _____ people

2. Joshua has 32 angelfish for every 12 snails he has. How many snails will he have when he has 72 angelfish?

   _____ _____ _____   _____

   _____

   _____

   Problem solution: _____ snails

3. Ann planted 35 rosebushes while Jim planted 14. How many rosebushes had Jim planted when Ann had planted 15?

   _____ _____ _____   _____

   _____

   Problem solution: _____ rosebushes

▶ Equivalent Factor Puzzles

Tell how these Factor Puzzles relate to each other
and to the proportion problems.

For each problem, Ann and Jim
plant rosebushes for the same
amount of time at their own
constant rates.

Factor Puzzle 1

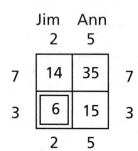

Ann   Jim
5   2

7 | 35 | 14 | 7
3 | 15 | 6 | 3

5   2

Proportion Problem 1

Ann planted 35 rosebushes while Jim
planted 14. When Ann had planted
15 rosebushes, how many had Jim
planted?

Factor Puzzle 2

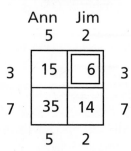

Jim   Ann
2   5

7 | 14 | 35 | 7
3 | 6 | 15 | 3

2   5

Proportion Problem 2

Jim planted 14 rosebushes while Ann
planted 35. How many rosebushes
had Jim planted when Ann had
planted 15?

Factor Puzzle 3

Ann   Jim
5   2

3 | 15 | 6 | 3
7 | 35 | 14 | 7

5   2

Proportion Problem 3

When Ann plants 15 rosebushes, how
many does Jim plant? Ann plants
35 rosebushes while Jim plants 14.

4. Write the tricky reversed question for each Factor Puzzle.

Factor Puzzle 1: _____

Factor Puzzle 2: _____

Factor Puzzle 3: _____

Identify and Solve Proportion Situations

▶ Numeric Proportions and Factor Puzzles

Show the Factor Puzzle for each proportion.

1. $a{:}32 = 15{:}40$

2. $16{:}36 = t{:}63$

3. $21{:}d = 27{:}18$

4. $27{:}45 :: 21{:}b$

5. $21{:}f :: 12{:}20$

6. $63{:}28 :: h{:}36$

▶ Patterns Within Proportions and Factor Puzzles

These proportions have been set up for you.
What patterns do you notice?

7. $2 \bullet 5 : 2 \bullet 12 =$
$13 \bullet 5 : 13 \bullet 12$

8. $2 \bullet 5 : 2 \bullet 67 =$
$39 \bullet 5 : 39 \bullet 67$

9. $a \bullet c : a \bullet d =$
$b \bullet c : b \bullet d$

	5	12
2	$2 \bullet 5$	$2 \bullet 12$
13	$13 \bullet 5$	$13 \bullet 12$

	5	67
2	$2 \bullet 5$	$2 \bullet 67$
39	$39 \bullet 5$	$39 \bullet 67$

	c	d
a	$a \bullet c$	$a \bullet d$
b	$b \bullet c$	$b \bullet d$

▶ Differentiate Proportion from Non-Proportion Problems

Circle the number of each problem that is a proportion problem and then solve it with a Factor Puzzle. Circle the basic ratio in each Factor Puzzle. If a problem is not a proportion problem, tell why.

Show your work.

10. Peachy Paint Company used 20 cans of blue and 15 cans of yellow paint to make Grasshopper Green paint. They have 8 more cans of blue paint. How many cans of yellow paint do they need to make more Grasshopper Green paint?

_____

_____

11. Mr. Tally's art class uses 2 bags of markers each week. Mr. Petro's art class uses 3 bags of markers one week, 2 bags the next week, and continues this pattern. If Mr. Tally used 14 bags of markers, how many did Mr. Petro use?

_____

_____

12. Jason keeps a constant ratio of minnows to goldfish in his pond. In the summer Jason's pond had 14 minnows for each 6 goldfish. Now it has 27 goldfish. How many minnows does it have now?

_____

_____

13. Tom is 12 years old. He is 8 years older than his sister Sylvia. How old were Tom and Sylvia 3 years ago?

_____

_____

Solve Numeric Proportion Problems

Name _____   Date _____

▶ Proportions with Basic Ratios

These proportions use a basic ratio. Show a simple solution on your MathBoard.

1. 2:3 :: 10:a

   a = _____

2. b:7 :: 20:28

   b = _____

3. What is the basic ratio

   for 21:35? _____

▶ Using the Greatest Common Factor

The **greatest common factor** of two whole numbers is the greatest whole number that divides into both numbers without any remainder.

The fastest way to find a basic ratio is to use the greatest common factor. But you can also find the basic ratio by using two or more steps.

4. Discuss Sam's and Asha's strategies for finding the basic ratio for 24:36.

Sam: I put 24 to 36 into a ratio table and divided both numbers by 6. Then I saw that I could divide the numbers in the new ratio 4 to 6 by 2 to get 2 to 3. No whole number (except 1) divides 2 and 3 evenly, so 2 to 3 is the basic ratio.

Asha: I know that 24 is 2 times 12 and 36 is 3 times 12, so 12 is a common factor. 24 and 36 could be in the 12s row of the multiplication table. So the basic ratio is 2 to 3.

÷ 2 ⤴ 2:3 ⤴ ÷ 2

4:6

÷ 6 ⤴ 24:36 ⤴ ÷ 6

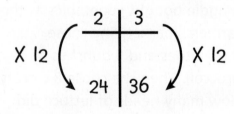

Solve. Show your work.

5. The basic ratio for 60:140 is

   _____ .

6. The basic ratio for 50:225 is

   _____ .

► Identify and Solve Basic Ratio Problems

Circle the number of the problem that is not a proportion problem and tell why it is not. Solve each proportion problem.

7. On one street, there are 2 dogs for every 5 cats. If 16 dogs live on the street, how many cats are there?

8. I have 60 blue marbles and 105 red marbles. What is the basic ratio of blue to red?

9. What is the basic ratio of blue to yellow for a paint mixture of 15 cans of blue paint and 21 cans of yellow paint?

10. Six of Susan's cookies weigh the same as 5 of Tara's cookies. How many of Susan's cookies weigh the same as 15 of Tara's cookies?

11. Maggie bought vegetables at the farmers' market. She chose 6 tomatoes and 9 bunches of broccoli. Then she chose 8 carrots. How many heads of lettuce did Maggie buy?

12. Andrew and Barbara begin collecting stamps at the same time. Every week Andrew adds 5 stamps to his collection and Barbara adds 7 to hers. How many stamps will Barbara have collected when Andrew has collected 30 stamps?

▶ Math and Hobbies

Model trains are miniature versions of actual trains. Some model trains are very small. The *scale* of a model is a ratio that compares the dimensions of a model train to the dimensions of an actual train.

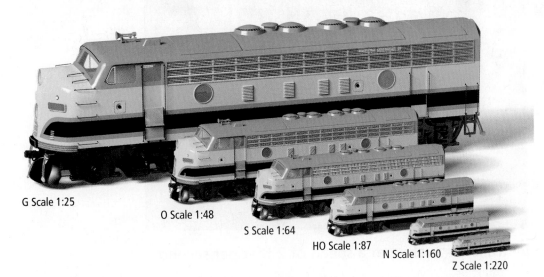

G Scale 1:25

O Scale 1:48

S Scale 1:64

HO Scale 1:87

N Scale 1:160

Z Scale 1:220

Train hobbyists use scale ratios and proportions to design layouts for their model trains. You can use scale ratios and proportions to find the dimensions of model train cars.

1. The Big Boy was a famous locomotive built during the 1940s. The locomotive was 132 feet long. About how long is an S-scale model of a Big Boy locomotive? (Hint: Use 128 feet instead of 132 feet for your estimate.)

2. The first American-built steam locomotive was about 159 inches long and nicknamed the Tom Thumb because it was so small. About how long is an N-scale model of a Tom Thumb locomotive?

3. An actual container railcar is 76 feet long. About how long is a G-scale model of a container railcar?

▶ Relate Time and Distance

Each year, the New York Botanical Garden displays a garden-scale model train.
The buildings are created from plant materials such as, seeds, bark, pods, and stems.

Suppose the model train is traveling at a speed of 2 feet per second.

4. Make a table to show how far the train travels in 5 seconds.

Time	Distance
Seconds	Feet
1	
2	
3	
4	
5	

5. Graph the relationship of time and distance.

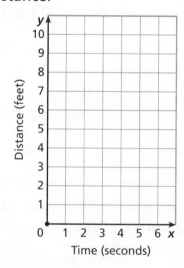

6. The bridge in the photo is about 3 times the height of the train. The buildings are about 4 times the height of the train. If the train cars are 6 inches tall, about how tall is each structure?

Focus on Mathematical Practices

Name _____   **Date** _____

▶ Vocabulary

Choose the best term from the box.

1. Two equivalent ratios make up a _____.
   (Lesson 1-10)

2. The ratio 4:6 is equivalent to the _____ 2:3.
   (Lessons 1-9, 1-13)

3. *Five oranges per bag* is a _____. (Lesson 1-4)

▶ Concepts and Skills

Complete.

4. Is this a proportion problem? Explain why or why not.

   > Gina puts 3 cups of nuts and 2 cups of raisins in
   > every batch of trail mix that she makes. If she
   > uses 12 cups of nuts, how many cups of raisins
   > will she use? (Lesson 1-12)

   _____

   _____

   _____

5. Use a picture to explain why 2:3 and 8:12 are equivalent
   ratios. (Lesson 1-8)

   _____

   _____

   _____

   _____

6. How do you know if a ratio is a *basic ratio*? (Lesson 1-13)

   _____

   _____

   _____

Name   Date

Solve each Factor Puzzle. (Lessons 1-1, 1-2)

7.

12	20
21	

8.

	63
40	35

Is the table a rate table? Write *Yes* or *No*. Explain how you know. (Lessons 1-4, 1-6, 1-7)

9.

Minutes	Miles
1	5
2	10
5	25
7	35
9	45

10.

Minutes	Miles
1	5
2	10
5	15
7	20
9	25

_____

_____

Use the rate table below for Exercises 11–14.

11. Complete the rate table.
    (Lessons 1-4, 1-6)

Pounds	Dollars
1	
	6
3	
4	12
	15

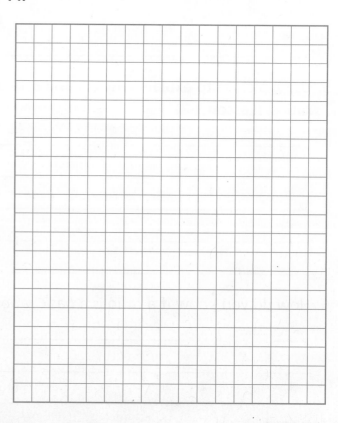

12. What is the unit rate for the table?
    (Lessons 1-3, 1-6)

    _____

13. Draw the graph for the rate table.
    (Lessons 1-6, 1-7)

14. Show the unit rate triangle on your
    graph. (Lessons 1-6, 1-7)

Complete each ratio table. Write the basic ratio in the top row. (Lesson 1-8)

15.

Roses	Daisies
⬭ : ⬭
: 4
6 :
9 : 12
: 16

16.

Apples	Oranges
⬭ : ⬭
5 :
10 : 14
: 21
20 :

Solve each proportion. (Lessons 1-12, 1-13)

17. 4:9 :: 12:*a*

18. *b*:10 :: 12:15

a = _____

b = _____

Write the basic ratio. (Lessons 1-13)

19. The basic ratio for 12:20 is _____.

Is the table a ratio table? Write *Yes* or *No*. If it is, write the basic ratio in the top row. (Lessons 1-9)

20. _____   Explain why the table is or is not a ratio table.

Pencils	Pens
⬭	⬭
7	6
14	12
21	24
28	38
35	42
42	48
49	56

_____

_____

_____

_____

_____

_____

▶ Problem Solving

Solve.

21. Tomatoes cost $2 per pound. What is the cost of 6 pounds of tomatoes? (Lesson 1-6)

_____

22. Melinda rides her bike at a constant speed. If she rides 18 miles in 2 hours, how far will she ride in 3 hours? (Lesson 1-7)

_____

23. Abby saves $3 per week and Luis saves $8 per week. How much will Abby have saved when Luis has saved $72? (Lesson 1-10)

_____

24. Greg mixes 6 cans of black paint with 8 cans of white paint to get a gray paint. How many cans of black paint will he need to mix with 48 cans of white paint to get the same gray color? (Lesson 1-11)

_____

25. **Extended Response** Write and solve a proportion word problem for this proportion:

$$6:10 = 21:d$$

(Lesson 1-12, 1-14)

_____

_____

_____

_____

_____

Family Letter

Dear Family,

Your student will be learning about geometry throughout the school year. This unit is about two kinds of measurement—perimeter and area. Perimeter is a measurement of length—the distance around a figure or an object. Area is a measurement of the amount of surface enclosed or covered by a figure or an object without gaps or overlaps.

We measure area in square units, such as square inches (in.^{2}) or square centimeters (cm^2).

1 in.^{2}

1 cm^2

Your student will learn to calculate the area and perimeter of these figures.

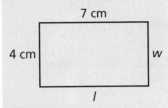
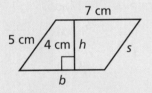
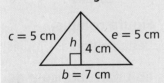

Rectangle
2 pairs of parallel sides
4 right angles

Parallelogram
2 pairs of parallel sides

Triangle
3 sides

Rhombus
2 pairs of parallel sides
4 sides the same length

Trapezoid
exactly one pair of parallel sides

Pentagon
5 sides

Hexagon
6 sides

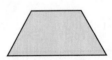

Octagon
8 sides

Complex Figure
composed of simpler figures

Students will also graph polygons on a coordinate grid to find side lengths using x– and y–coordinates and to find perimeter and area.

If you have any questions or comments, please call or write to me.

Sincerely,
Your child's teacher

COMMON CORE   This unit includes the Common Core Standards for Mathematical Content for Geometry and Algebra, 6.G.1, 6.G.3, 6.EE.2, 6.EE.2.c, 6.EE.3, 6.EE.4

Carta a la familia

Estimada familia:

Durante el año escolar, su hijo aprenderá geometría. En esta unidad estudiaremos dos tipos de mediciones: perímetro y área. El perímetro, que es una medición de longitud, es la distancia que rodea a una figura o un objeto. El área es la medición de la superficie que cubre un objeto sin espacios ni traslapos.

Medimos el área en unidades cuadradas, como pulgadas cuadradas (pulg²) o centímetros cuadrados (cm²).

1 pulg²

1 cm²

Su hijo aprenderá a calcular el área y el perímetro de estas figuras.

Calcular el perímetro y el área

Rectángulo

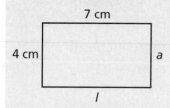

7 cm

4 cm

a

l

Perímetro = $2l + 2a$
Perímetro = $2 \times 7 + 2 \times 4$
Perímetro = $14 + 8 = 22$
Perímetro = 22 cm

Área = $l \times a$
Área = $7 \times 4 = 28$
Área = 28 cm²

Paralelogramo

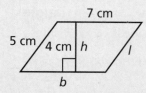

7 cm

5 cm   4 cm h l

b

Perímetro = $2b + 2l$
Perímetro = $2 \times 7 + 2 \times 5$
Perímetro = $14 + 10 = 24$
Perímetro = 24 cm

Área = $b \times h$
Área = $7 \times 4 = 28$
Área = 28 cm²

Triángulo

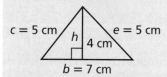

$c = 5$ cm h $e = 5$ cm
   4 cm
$b = 7$ cm

Perímetro = $c + b + e$
Perímetro = $5 + 7 + 5 = 17$
Perímetro = 17 cm

Área = $\frac{1}{2} b \times h$
Área = $\frac{1}{2} (7 \times 4)$
Área = 14 cm²

  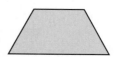

Rectángulo
2 pares de lados paralelos
4 ángulos rectos

Paralelogramo
2 pares de lados paralelos

Triángulo
3 lados

Rombo
2 pares de lados paralelos
4 lados del mismo largo

Trapecio
exactamente un par
de lados paralelos

Pentágono
5 lados

Hexágono
6 lados

Octágono
8 lados

Figura compleja
compuesta de figuras simples

Los estudiantes también trazarán polígonos en una cuadrícula de coordenadas, usando las coordenadas $x-$ y $y-$ para hallar el largo de los lados, el perímetro y el área.

Si tiene alguna pregunta, por favor comuníquese conmigo.

Atentamente,
El maestro de su hijo

COMMON CORE   Esta unidad incluye los Common Core Standards for Mathematical Content for Geometry and Algebra, 6.G.1, 6.G.3, 6.EE.2, 6.EE.2.c, 6.EE.3, 6.EE.4

Name _____ Date _____

Vocabulary

perimeter
area
square centimeter (cm²)

▶ Formulas for Perimeter and Area

1. Look at the rectangles below.
   What does **perimeter** mean?
   What does **area** mean?

   _____

   _____

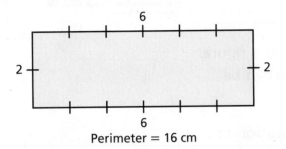

Perimeter = 16 cm

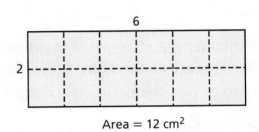

Area = 12 cm²

On your MathBoard, draw a rectangle for each
Exercise 2–5. Mark each centimeter with a tick mark, and
write an equation that shows how to find the perimeter.
Then outline and shade the **square centimeters** (cm²)
and write an equation that shows how to find the area.

	Length	Width	Perimeter	Area
	6 cm	2 cm	2 + 6 + 2 + 6 = 16 P = 16 cm	6 × 2 = 12 A = 12 cm²
2.	4 cm	3 cm		
3.	8 cm	1 cm		
4.	5 cm	5 cm		
5.	10 cm	4 cm		
6.	l	w		

The last row of the table should show your formulas for perimeter and area.

▶ Perimeter and Area of a Square

The figure at the right is a square. The length of one side of the square is given.

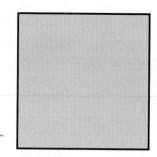

76 cm

7. Explain why you know the lengths of the other three sides of the square.

_____

_____

8. Perimeter is a measure of the distance around a figure. In the space at the right, show how addition can be used to find the perimeter of the square.

9. In the space at the right, show how multiplication can be used to find the perimeter.

10. **Discuss** To calculate the area of a rectangle, we find the product of the measures of two of its adjacent sides. Why can this formula also be used to find the area of a square?

11. In the space at the right, calculate the area of the square. Then write a formula for the area of a square.

_____

Solve.

12. How does doubling each dimension of a rectangle that is not a square affect the perimeter and the area of that rectangle? Give an example to support your answer.

_____

_____

13. How does doubling each dimension of a square affect the perimeter and the area of that square? Give an example to support your answer.

_____

_____

▶ What's the Error?

Dear Math Students,

Today I went to the paint store to buy paint for my dining room ceiling.

My ceiling is a rectangle 12 feet long and 10 feet wide. I told the clerk that I needed enough paint to cover 120 feet. He told me that I'd made a mistake.

Can you tell me what I did wrong?

Your friend,

Puzzled Penguin

14. Write a response to the Puzzled Penguin.

_____

_____

_____

Dear Math Students,

It looks like I need your help again. I am sewing some fringe along the edge of a tablecloth. The tablecloth is a rectangle 96 inches long and 54 inches wide. I bought 150 inches of fringe. I started to sew on the fringe, but I ran out before I finished!

What did I do wrong in my calculation? How much fringe do I need to go around the whole tablecloth?

Your friend,

Puzzled Penguin

15. Write a response to the Puzzled Penguin.

_____

_____

▶ Find the Side Length or Area

Find the side length or area of each rectangle or square.

16.
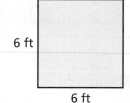
6 ft

6 ft

A = _____

17.
s | A = 25 in.²

s

s = _____

18.
2 in. | A = 12 in.²

b

b = _____

19.
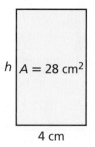
h | A = 28 cm²

4 cm

h = _____

20.
1 yd

8 yd

A = _____

21.
b

3 ft | A = 18 ft²

b = _____

▶ Solve Word Problems

22. Stephen drew a picture of his sister that is 8 cm long and 5 cm wide. He wants to make a frame out of colored tape to put around the picture. How much tape will he need?

_____

23. Ben wants to tile a patio. Each tile is a square and has an area of 1 ft². How many tiles will it take to cover a patio that is 5 ft by 7 ft?

_____

24. Janine ordered 200 square feet of carpeting to cover the floor of her rectangular family room. The length of the family room is 20 feet. How wide is it?

_____

Vocabulary

height
base

▶ Perimeter and Area of a Right Triangle

1. What is the area of the rectangle shown here?

   _____

2. Draw a diagonal line and make two triangles.
   What is the area of each triangle?
   Why do you think so?

   _____

   _____

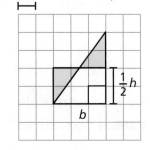

3 cm

6 cm

3. What do you notice about the two yellow triangles?

   _____

   _____

1 cm

$\frac{1}{2}h$

b

4. How do the areas of the rectangle and the large
   right triangle compare? Explain your reasoning.

   _____

   _____

5. Write and use a formula to find the area of the
   rectangle or the large right triangle above.

   _____

6. Do the rectangle and large triangle at the right
   have the same areas? Explain how you know.

   _____

   _____

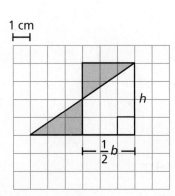

1 cm

h

$\frac{1}{2}b$

7. Write and use a formula to find the area of the
   large right triangle to the right.

   _____

Vocabulary

right triangle
related rectangle

A triangle with a right angle (square corner) is called a **right triangle**. The area of any right triangle is half the area of a rectangle with the same base and height or the same area as a rectangle with $\frac{1}{2}$ the base or height. These rectangles are called **related rectangles**.

What is the area of each right triangle shown below?

8.
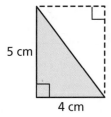

5 cm

4 cm

A = _____

9.
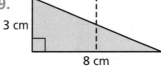

3 cm

8 cm

A = _____

10.
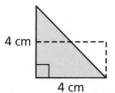

4 cm

4 cm

A = _____

To show that a triangle is a right triangle, mark the right angle with a small box. Find the area of each right triangle below.

11.
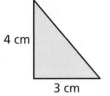

4 cm

3 cm

A = _____

12.
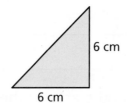

6 cm

6 cm

A = _____

13.
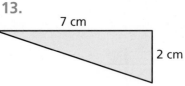

7 cm

2 cm

A = _____

14.
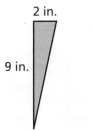

2 in.

9 in.

A = _____

15.
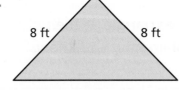

8 ft   8 ft

A = _____

16.
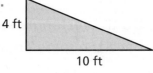

4 ft

10 ft

A = _____

17. This right triangle has sides of length *c*, *d*, and *e*. Write a formula for the area of any right triangle.

_____

18. Write a formula for the perimeter of any right triangle.

_____

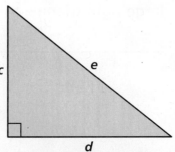

c

e

d

▶ What's the Error?

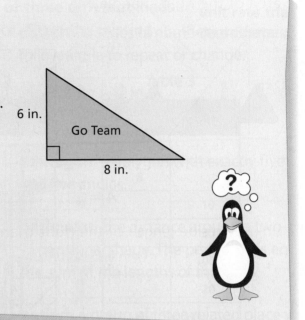

Dear Math Students,

Today I found the area of a pennant that is in the shape of a right triangle with a base of 8 in. and a height of 6 in. Here is how I found the answer.

$A = \frac{1}{2} bh = 6 \times 8 = 48 \quad A = 48$ in.^{2}

So, the area of the pennant is 48 in.^{2}

Am I correct? If not, please correct my work and explain below.

Your friend,

Puzzled Penguin

6 in.

Go Team

8 in.

19. Write a response to the Puzzled Penguin.

_____

_____

_____

_____

_____

20. Show two ways to multiply to compute the area of the right triangle.

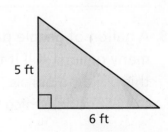

5 ft

6 ft

_____

_____

_____

_____

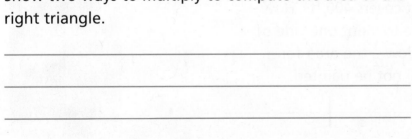

▶ Find the Area

Find the area of the right triangle.

21.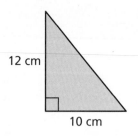

$A =$ _____

22.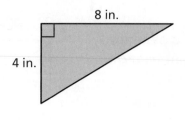
8 in.

$A =$ _____

23.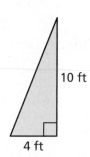
10 ft

4 ft

$A =$ _____

Find the unknown side length of the right triangle.

24.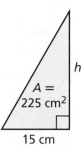
h

$A = 225\ cm^2$

15 cm

$h =$ _____

25. 20 in.
$A = 200\ in.^2$
h

$h =$ _____

26.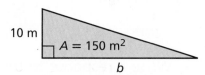
10 m
$A = 150\ m^2$
b

$b =$ _____

Solve.

27. How much fabric is needed to make two sails?

_____

14 ft
Sail

8 ft

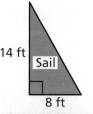

28. A gallon of purple paint covers 400 ft². How many gallons will it take to paint one side of this building purple? Allow $\frac{1}{2}$ the area for the windows, which will not be painted.

_____

_____

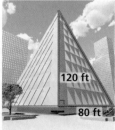
120 ft

80 ft

29. A plot of land is in the shape of a right triangle. The plot has an area of 2,400 square feet. The base is 80 ft. What is the height?

_____

▶ Experiment with Parallelograms

The **height** of a **parallelogram** is a line segment that is **perpendicular** to the **base**.

Cut out each pair of parallelograms below and then cut along the dashed line segment that shows each height. Switch the pieces. Put the slanted ends together.

What figure do you form?

_____

Do you think it will always happen when the height connects the base and the opposite side? Why or why not?

_____

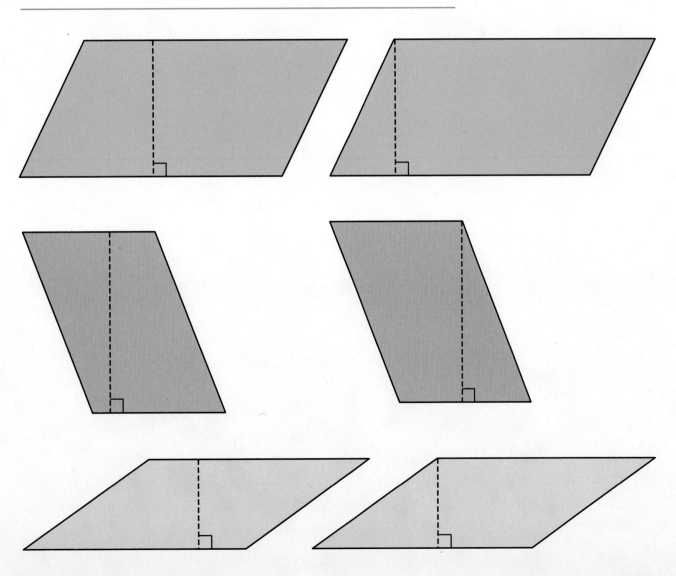

Area of Any Parallelogram

▶ Erica's Solution

Here is how Erica found the area of a parallelogram with
no vertices over the base.

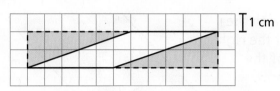

Area of Rectangle − Area of Two Right Triangles = Area of Parallelogram

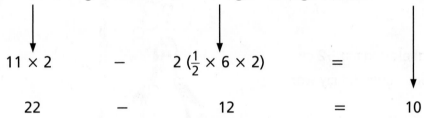

$$11 \times 2 \qquad - \qquad 2\left(\tfrac{1}{2} \times 6 \times 2\right) \qquad =$$

$$22 \qquad - \qquad 12 \qquad = \qquad 10$$

So, the area of the parallelogram is 10 cm².

1. Can you compute the area of the parallelogram above
   using the formula $A = bh$? Explain.

   _____

   _____

Find the area of the parallelogram. Show your work.

2.

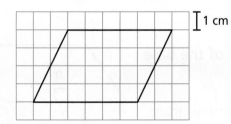

_____

$A =$ _____

3.

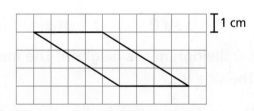

_____

$A =$ _____

▶ What's the Error?

Dear Math Students,

Today I made a design with the parallelogram shown at the right. Then I found the area of the parallelogram. Here is how I found my answer.

$A = \text{base} \times \text{height}$

$A = 6 \times 7 = 42$

So, the area of the parallelogram is 42 cm².

Am I correct? If not, please correct my work and explain below.

Your friend,

Puzzled Penguin

5 cm   7 cm

6 cm

4. Write a response to the Puzzled Penguin.

_____

_____

▶ Find the Area of a Parallelogram

This parallelogram has height *h*. The measurement of the base is *b*. The side is *s*.

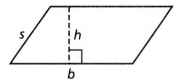

5. Write a formula for finding the area of the parallelogram.

_____

6. What measurement shown is not used for finding the area?

_____

7. Write a formula to find the perimeter of the parallelogram.

_____

8. What measurement shown is not used for finding the perimeter?

_____

Vocabulary

rhombus

▶ Find the Area of a Rhombus

A **rhombus** is a parallelogram with all sides the same length.

Place a check mark next to each rhombus. Then find the perimeter and area of each figure.

9.

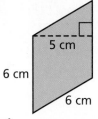

5 cm

6 cm

6 cm

A = _____

P = _____

10.

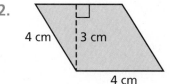

3 cm   4 cm

7 cm

A = _____

P = _____

11.

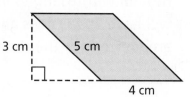

3 cm   5 cm

4 cm

A = _____

P = _____

12.

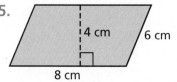

4 cm   3 cm

4 cm

A = _____

P = _____

13.

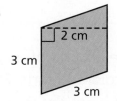

2 cm

3 cm

3 cm

A = _____

P = _____

14.

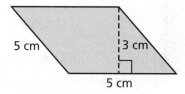

5 cm   3 cm

5 cm

A = _____

P = _____

15.

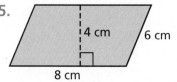

4 cm   6 cm

8 cm

A = _____

P = _____

16.

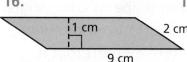

1 cm   2 cm

9 cm

A = _____

P = _____

17.

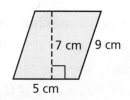

7 cm   9 cm

5 cm

A = _____

P = _____

Solve.

18. A rhombus has a base of 11 cm and an area of 110 cm².
What is the height of the rhombus?

_____

19. What is the area of the rhombus at the right?
Explain how you computed the area.

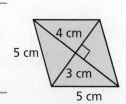

4 cm

5 cm

3 cm

5 cm

_____

_____

▶ Solve Real World Problems

Solve.

Show your work

20. Jun is designing a pattern for a rug. She will use rhombi with triangles in between. Each rhombus will have 10 in. sides and a 9 in. height. What is the area of four of the rhombi?

21. Haig is ordering a pool cover that is in the shape of a parallelogram. The cover has a base of 40 ft and a height of 20 ft. The cost of the cover is $4 per ft². What is the cost of the pool cover?

22. Deirdre is making a design for the bottom of a dress using rhombi cut from different colored fabric. Each rhombus has a base of 3 in. and a height of 2 in. How much blue fabric does she need for 12 rhombi?

23. Lionel is making shelves in the shape of a rectangle. Each shelf will be 8 in. long and 11 in. wide. How many shelves can be made from a board that is 8 in. wide and 8 ft long?

24. The height of a right triangle is four times the height of another right triangle. The lengths of the bases of the two triangles are equal. How do the areas of the triangles compare?

25. Lin's backyard is a square that has a perimeter of 120 feet. What is the area of his backyard?

▶ Experiment with Triangles

The acute triangles below are exactly the same. Cut them out
and rotate one so that you can place sides labeled *a* together.
What shape do you form? Do the same with sides labeled *b* and *c*.

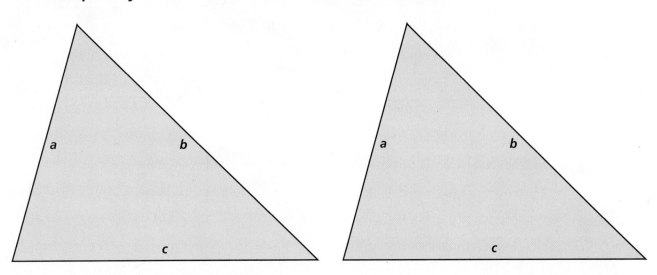

The obtuse triangles below are exactly the same. Cut them out
and rotate one so that you can place sides labeled *x* together.
What shape do you form? Do the same with sides labeled *y* and *z*.

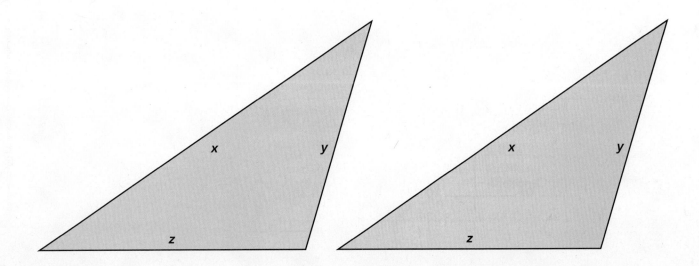

Name _____   Date _____

▶ Draw Parallelograms and Triangles

Answer the following questions about triangle *ABC*.

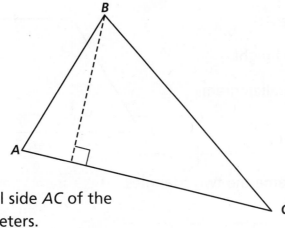

1. Measure and label side *AC* of the triangle in centimeters.

2. Measure and label the height.

3. What is the area of the triangle?

   _____

4. Use your ruler to draw a line segment through *B* that is parallel to *AC*.

5. Draw a line segment through *C* that is parallel to *AB*. Label point *D* where the two new line segments meet.

6. A **related parallelogram** has the same base and height as its related triangle or rectangle. What is the area of related parallelogram *ABDC*?

   _____

7. Use the directions in Exercises 1–6 for this obtuse triangle.

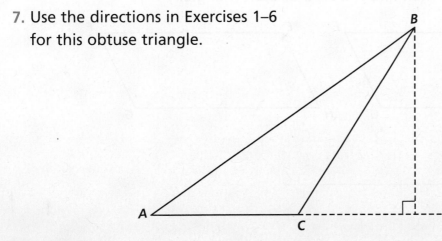

▶ Draw Parallelograms and Triangles (continued)

Complete.

8. Measure and label side *AD*.

9. Measure and label the height.

10. What is the area of parallelogram
    ABCD?

_____

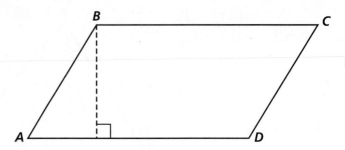

11. Join points *B* and *D*. Name the two triangles.

_____

12. What is the area of each triangle?

_____

13. What kind of triangles did you make in
    Exercise 11?

_____

14. Divide parallelogram *ABCD* into
    two obtuse triangles.

15. What is the area of each obtuse triangle?

_____

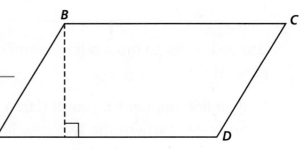

16. Draw two different diagonals for parallelogram *EFGH*. Name
    the triangles. Measure, then find the area of each triangle.

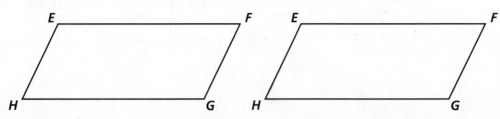

_____

_____

Area of Any Triangle

Name _____ Date _____

Vocabulary

area
base
height
vertex

▶ Calculate the Area of a Triangle

Answer the following.

17. How does the area of the shaded triangle compare to the area of the parallelogram?

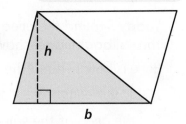

_____

18. What measurements do you need to know to find the area of any triangle?

_____

_____

19. Write a formula for the area of any triangle.

_____

The parallelogram and the shaded triangle shown here both have a base of 4 cm and a height of 3 cm.

20. What is the area of the parallelogram?

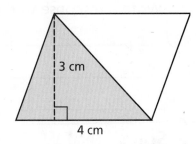

_____

21. What is the area of the triangle?

_____

The height of a triangle is a line segment drawn from a vertex perpendicular to the base. Sometimes the base has to be extended to draw the height.

Point *A* is a **vertex** of triangle *ADC*.

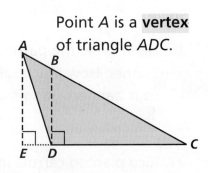

22. Which line segment shows the height of triangle *ADC*?

_____

23. Which line segment shows the height of triangle *XYZ*?

_____

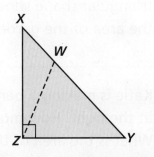

24. How are the heights of acute, obtuse, and right triangles alike and different?

_____

_____

▶ What's the Error?

Dear Math Students,

Today I found the area of the sail on the sailboat model shown at the right.

Here is how I found the answer.

$A = 6 \times 7 = 42$ $A = 42$ cm²

So, the area of the sail is 42 cm².

Am I correct? If not, please correct my work and explain below.

Your friend,

Puzzled Penguin

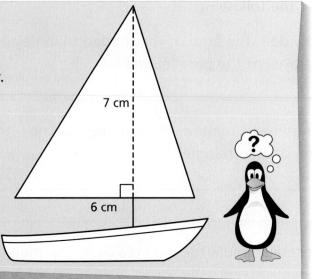

7 cm

6 cm

25. Write a response to the Puzzled Penguin.

_____

_____

_____

▶ Solve Real World Problems

Solve.

26. Heidi drew the pattern at the right for making a banner. How much felt will she need to make four banners using this pattern?

_____

27. Rico planted carrots in his garden in the triangular shape shown at the right. What is the area of the garden planted with carrots?

_____

28. Katie is making a pen for her pigs as shown at the right. How much fence will she need? What is the area of the pen?

_____

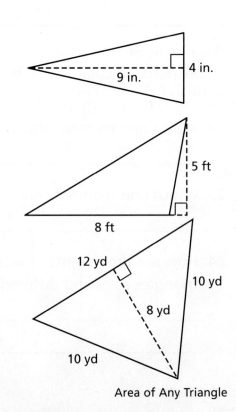

9 in.   4 in.

5 ft

8 ft

12 yd   10 yd

8 yd

10 yd

Area of Any Triangle

Vocabulary

dimensions

▶ Select Appropriate Measurements

Discuss the **dimensions** you need to find the perimeter of a triangle.

Figure A	Figure B	Figure C

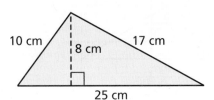

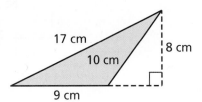

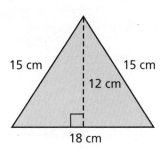

Find the perimeter of each triangle.

1. Figure A _____ 2. Figure B _____ 3. Figure C _____

Discuss the dimensions you need to find the area of a triangle.
Find the area of each triangle.

4. Figure A _____ 5. Figure B _____ 6. Figure C _____

Discuss the dimensions you need to find the perimeter and area of a parallelogram.

Figure D	Figure E	Figure F

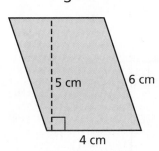

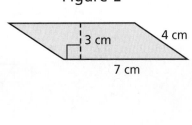

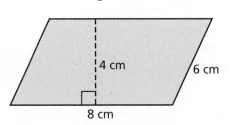

Find the perimeter of each parallelogram.

7. Figure D _____ 8. Figure E _____ 9. Figure F _____

Find the area of each parallelogram.

10. Figure D _____ 11. Figure E _____ 12. Figure F _____

▶ Choose a Base

Choose a base and a corresponding height with lengths
you can find without a ruler. Then find the area. Each
square represents 1 cm².

13.

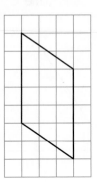

A = _____

14.

A = _____

15.

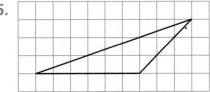

A = _____

16.

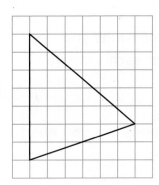

A = _____

17.

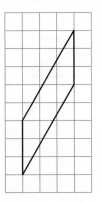

A = _____

18.

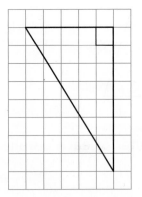

A = _____

▶ Practice Finding Perimeter and Area

Find the perimeter **and the area** **of each figure.**

19.

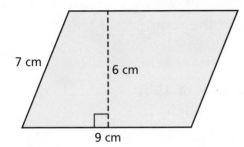

P = _____

A = _____

20.

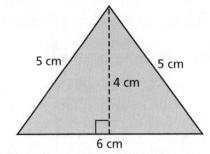

P = _____

A = _____

21.

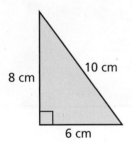

P = _____

A = _____

22.

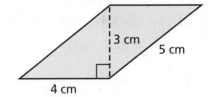

P = _____

A = _____

23.

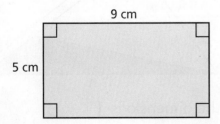

P = _____

A = _____

24.

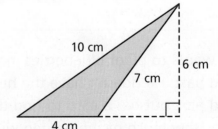

P = _____

A = _____

▶ Solve Real World Problems

Solve. Draw a picture to help you.

25. An attic playroom floor is in the shape of a rhombus with a base of 12 ft and a height of 6 ft. How much carpeting is needed? How much wood molding is needed to go around the room?

_____

26. A dining room with a rectangular shape has a length of 15 ft and a width of 10 ft. A wallpaper border will be placed around the room. How much wallpaper border will be needed? How much wallpaper will be needed to cover the ceiling?

_____

Use the drawing of the flag at the right for Problems 27 and 28.

27. A ribbon of looped fastener will be sewn around the edge of the back of the flag. How much looped fastener is needed?

_____

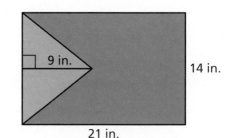

9 in.   14 in.

21 in.

28. How much of the flag is blue?

_____

Use the drawing at the right for Problems 29–30.

29. David has a garden in the shape shown at the right. He wants to put a fence all the way around the garden. How much fencing will David need?

_____

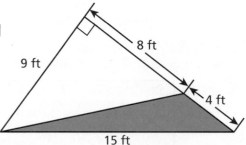

8 ft

9 ft

4 ft

15 ft

30. David wants to plant blueberries in the shaded part. He doesn't have the height of the shaded part but has a plan to find the area with the dimensions he has. How much of the garden will be sunflowers?

_____

▶ Experiment with Trapezoids

A **trapezoid** is a quadrilateral with exactly one pair of parallel sides. Cut out the trapezoids below. Then cut each trapezoid along the dashed line to form two triangles. How do the base and height of the two triangles compare to the bases and height of the trapezoid?

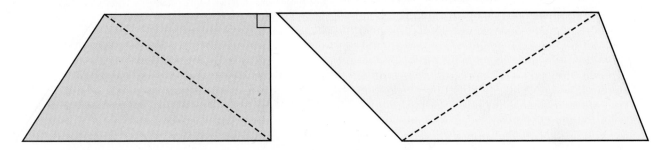

The trapezoids below are exactly the same. Cut them out and rotate one so that you can place sides labeled *a* together. What shape do you form?

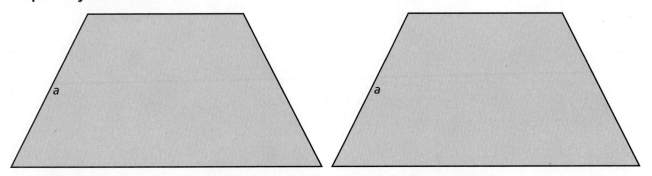

The trapezoid below has a midline that connects the midpoints of the slanted sides. Measure the length of the midline and the lengths of the bases of the trapezoid. How does the length of the midline compare with the sum of the bases? Cut out the trapezoid. Then cut along the dashed lines and turn the triangles to form a rectangle.

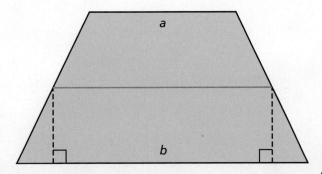

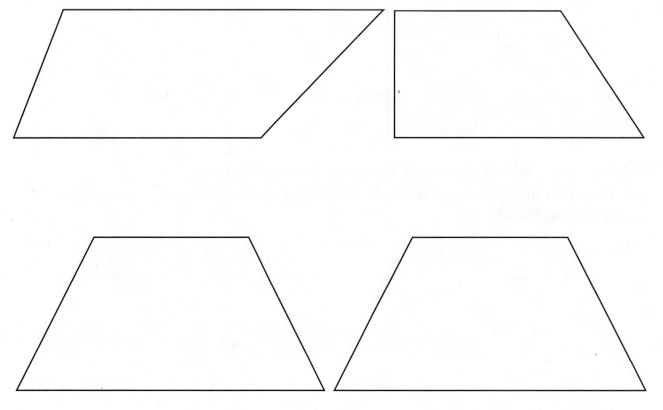

Area of Any Trapezoid

Name _____   Date _____

▶ Experiment with Trapezoids (continued)

Cut each isosceles trapezoid along the dashed line. Flip one piece over. Put the pieces together to form a four-sided figure with opposite sides parallel. What figure do you form? Then put the pieces together another way to form another figure with opposite sides parallel and four right angles. What figure do you form?

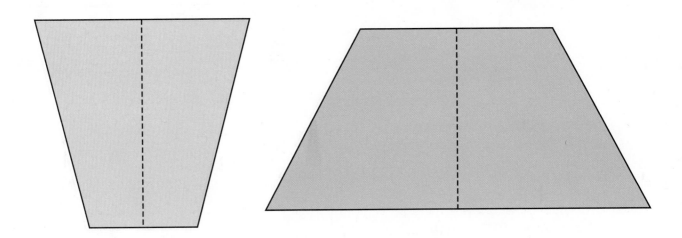

The height of a trapezoid is a perpendicular segment between its parallel bases. Draw two heights in each isosceles trapezoid. Place your heights so that you make three figures for which you know area formulas. What shapes did you form?

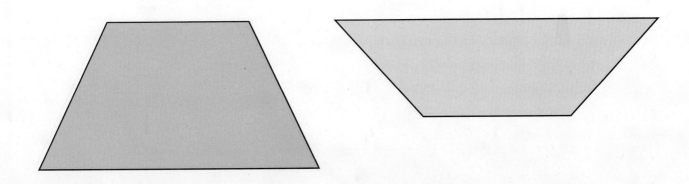

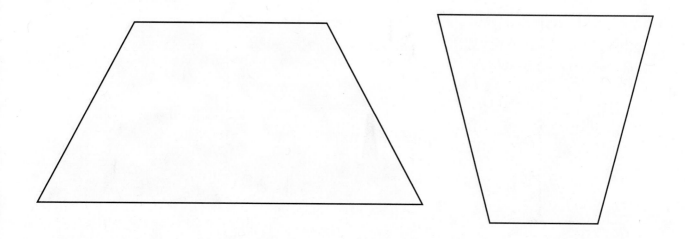

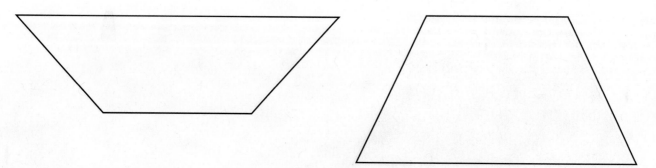

Area of Any Trapezoid

▶ Calculate the Area of a Trapezoid

Toshi divided a trapezoid into two triangles and labeled the height and bases as shown.

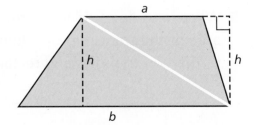

1. What formula could you write for the area of the trapezoid by adding the areas of the two triangles?

_____

Kaia put two copies of an isosceles trapezoid together to form a parallelogram and labeled the height and bases as shown.

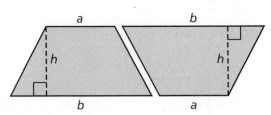

2. What formula could you write for the area of one trapezoid using a formula for the parallelogram?

_____

Jorge drew a line segment that connects the midpoints of the slanted sides. Then cut and flipped the triangles to form a rectangle.

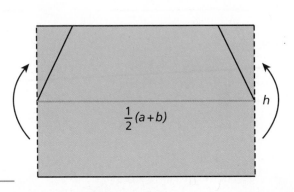

3. What formula could you write for the area of the trapezoid using a formula for the rectangle that was formed?

_____

Robert cut an isosceles trapezoid into two pieces, flipped one piece and joined them to make a parallelogram.

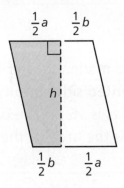

4. What formula could you write for the area of the trapezoid, using a formula for the parallelogram?

_____

Name _____ **Date** _____

Ana divided an isosceles trapezoid into two triangles and a rectangle.

5. What formula could you write for the area of the trapezoid by adding the areas of the two triangles and rectangle?

_____

_____

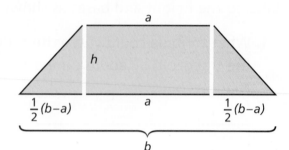

▶ Find the Area of a Trapezoid

Find the area.

6.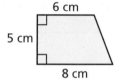
6 cm
5 cm
8 cm

_____

7.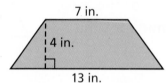
7 in.
4 in.
13 in.

_____

8.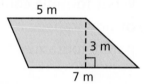
5 m
3 m
7 m

_____

9.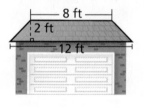
8 ft
2 ft
12 ft

_____

10.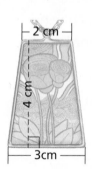
2 cm
4 cm
3cm

_____

11.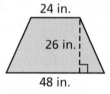
24 in.
26 in.
48 in.

_____

Solve.

12. Priscilla made a poster in the shape of a trapezoid and folded the slanted sides into two right triangles. The height of the triangles is 16 in. The bases of the trapezoid are 12 in. and 24 in. What is the area of the trapezoid?

_____

13. Carlos made a design for a kite in the shape of a trapezoid. The parallel sides are 6 in. and 36 in. The height is 34 in. How much fabric will it take to make two kites using this design?

_____

Area of Any Trapezoid

▶ Visualize Figures

1. Find the area of the triangle.

_____

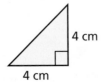

4 cm

4 cm

2. Find the area of the rectangle.

_____

3. Find the area of the **complex figure**.

_____

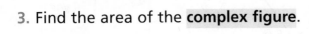

4 cm

6 cm

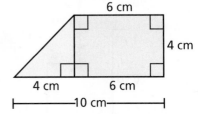

6 cm

4 cm

4 cm   6 cm

10 cm

▶ Find Area and Perimeter of Complex Figures

Find the area and perimeter of these complex figures.

4.

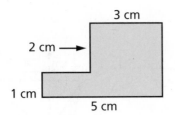

3 cm

2 cm →

1 cm

5 cm

P = _____

A = _____

5.

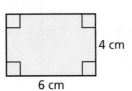

5 cm

8 cm   10 cm

11 cm

P = _____

A = _____

6.

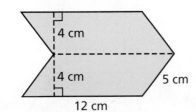

4 cm

4 cm   5 cm

12 cm

P = _____

A = _____

7.

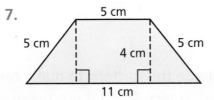

5 cm

5 cm   5 cm

4 cm

11 cm

P = _____

A = _____

8. Vadim needs to know the area of this complex figure,
so he calls his friend Serena. Serena says she can figure
out the area if Vadim will make just three measurements.
Which three measurements does Vadim need to make?

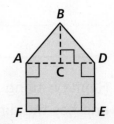

B

A   D
   C

F   E

_____

▶ Find Area and Perimeter of Complex Figures (continued)

Find the perimeter and area.

9.
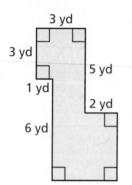
3 yd

3 yd

1 yd

5 yd

2 yd

6 yd

10.
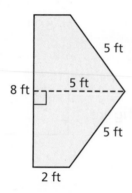
5 ft

5 ft

8 ft

5 ft

2 ft

11.
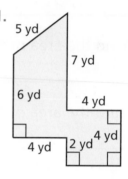
5 yd

7 yd

6 yd

4 yd

4 yd

2 yd

4 yd

P = _____ A = _____   P = _____ A = _____   P = _____ A = _____

▶ Strategies for Finding Area

Find the area of the shaded part.

12.
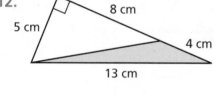
8 cm

5 cm

4 cm

13 cm

13.
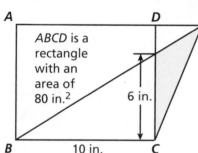
A   *D*

ABCD is a rectangle with an area of 80 in.²

6 in.

B   10 in.   *C*

14.
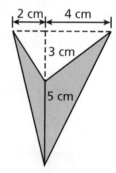
2 cm   4 cm

3 cm

5 cm

_____   _____   _____

15. Monique made this pattern to make cards to label her Science Fair project. She did not measure the height of the card, but says she can find the area with these measurements. Is she correct? Explain.

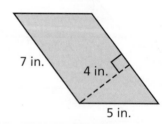
7 in.

4 in.

5 in.

_____

_____

_____

16. Haime is tiling a patio that is in the shape of a kite and has the dimensions shown at the right. How many square feet of tiles does he need?

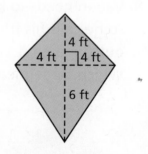
4 ft

4 ft   4 ft

6 ft

_____

Area of a Complex Figure

► Area of a Regular Pentagon

1. How many same-size isosceles triangles are inside the regular **pentagon**?

   _____

2. Measure the base and the height of the isosceles triangle to the nearest centimeter.

   _____

3. What is the area of the triangle to the nearest cm²?

   _____

4. What is the area of the pentagon to the nearest cm²?

   _____

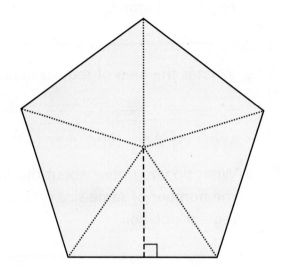

► Area of a Regular Hexagon

5. Estimate the area of the regular **hexagon** by finding the area of the isosceles triangle. Show your work.

   _____

   _____

   _____

   _____

   _____

   _____

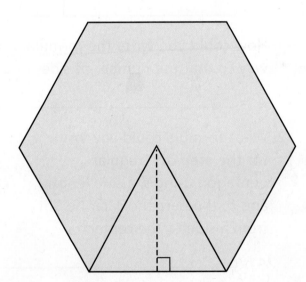

6. The height of the triangle is rounded to the nearest cm. Find the area of regular hexagon *ABCDEF* using the measurements given.

   _____

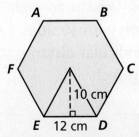

A   B

F   C

10 cm

E   12 cm   D

Name   Date

▶ Area of a Regular Octagon

7. How many same-size isosceles triangles are in a regular **octagon**?

_____

8. What is the area of regular octagon *ABCDEFGH*?

_____

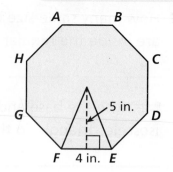

▶ Area of Any Regular Polygon

9. What do you notice about the number of sides and the number of same-size isosceles triangles inside a regular polygon?

_____

10. What formula could you write for the area of a regular octagon using *s*, a side length, and *h*, the perpendicular height from a side to the center.

    $A =$ _____

Regular Octagon Triangles
$A = bh$

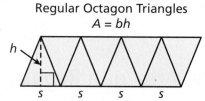

11. How could you write the formula, A = 4*sh*, another way so that the number of sides in an octagon is used?

    $A =$ _____

12. What formula could you write for the area of a regular pentagon using *s*, a side length, and *h*, the perpendicular height from a side to the center?

    Regular Pentagon Triangles
    $A = \frac{1}{2}bh$

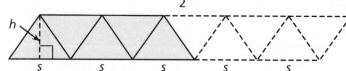

    $A =$ _____

13. Write a formula for the area of a regular polygon with *n* sides. Use the formula to find the area of a regular polygon with 10 sides. Each side measures 8 in. and the perpendicular distance to the center is 12 in. to the nearest inch.

    $A =$ _____

Vocabulary

coordinates

▶ Plot a Polygon

1. On the grid at the right, plot a polygon that you can find the area of with an even number of units for the base (or bases) and height. The vertices should be located so that they can be named by whole-number coordinates.

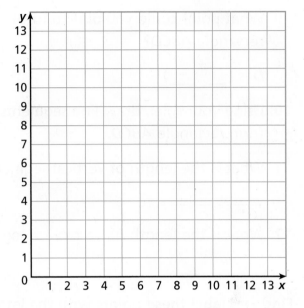

2. What polygon did you plot?

_____

3. Name the coordinates of the vertices of your polygon.

_____

4. Find the area of your polygon.

_____

5. On the grid at the right, plot another polygon that is the same shape as the polygon above. The base (or bases) and height of the new polygon should be half as long as in the polygon above.

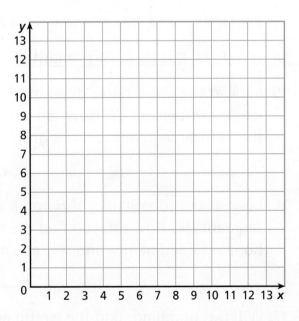

6. Name the coordinates of the vertices of your polygon.

_____

7. Find the area of your new polygon.

_____

8. How does the area of the polygon you drew for Problem 1 compare to the one you drew for Problem 5?

_____

Name _____   Date _____

▶ Find Segment Lengths

9. What point could you plot to form rectangle *ABCD*?

   D is (___ , ___)

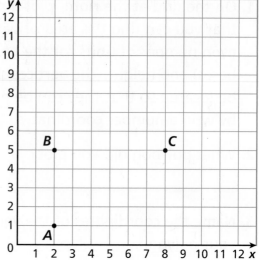

10. Using your ruler, draw line segments to form rectangle *ABCD*.

11. What is the length of vertical segment *AB*?

   _____

12. What is the length of horizontal segment *BC*?

   _____

Find and label these points with the letter and coordinates given. Then connect the points and find the segment length.

13. *E* is (1, 9). *F* is (1, 12). The length of *EF* is _____.

14. *H* is (6, 8). *K* is (8, 8). The length of *HK* is _____.

15. Look at the coordinates of points *E* and *F* and the length of segment *EF*. How can you find the length of this vertical segment without graphing?

   _____

16. Look at the coordinates of *H* and *K* and the length of segment *HK*. How can you find the length of this horizontal segment without graphing?

   _____

17. Without graphing, find the length and direction of a line segment with endpoints at (12, 10) and (12, 2).

   _____

18. Without graphing, find the length and direction of a line segment with endpoints at (0, 7) and (6, 7).

   _____

Graph Polygons in the Coordinate Plane

▶ Find Perimeters and Areas of Polygons in the Coordinate Plane

19. The length of line segment *AC* is 6 units. Label the coordinates of point *C* without counting spaces.

20. Using a ruler, draw line segments connecting points *A*, *B*, and *C* to form a polygon. What polygon did you form?

_____

21. Segment *BC* is 10 units long. Find the perimeter and area of right triangle *ABC*.

    P = _____

    A = _____

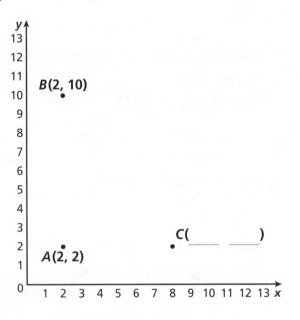

22. Using a ruler, draw line segments to form polygon *DEFH*. What polygon did you form?

_____

23. Segment *FH* is 8 units long. Label the coordinates of point *F* without counting spaces.

24. Segment *EF* is 13 units long. Find the perimeter and area of parallelogram *DEFH*.

    P = _____

    A = _____

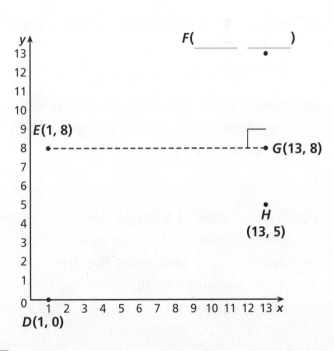

► Find Perimeters and Areas of Polygons in the Coordinate Plane (continued)

25. Plot these points on the coordinate plane at the right.
K(2, 3), L(5, 7), M(13, 7)

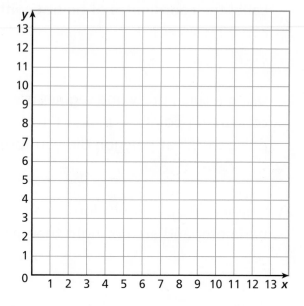

26. Using a ruler, connect your points with line segments to form a polygon. What polygon did you form?

_____

27. Segment KL is 5 units long. Segment KM is 12 units long to the nearest whole unit. Find the perimeter and area of triangle KLM to the nearest whole unit.

P = _____

A = _____

28. Plot these points on the coordinate plane at the right.
A(2, 1), B(6, 7), C(12, 3)

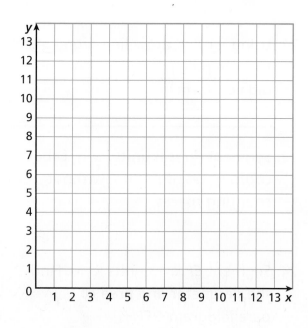

29. Using a ruler, connect your points with line segments to form a polygon. What polygon did you form?

_____

30. Find the area of triangle ABC.
Hint: Enclose the triangle in a rectangle and take away the areas of the surrounding right triangles. Show your work.

_____

_____

_____

Graph Polygons in the Coordinate Plane

▶ Solve Real World Problems

31. A surveyor marked the border of a property with metal pins at these coordinates on a survey map.

    A(1, 1), B(1, 10), C(7, 10), D(13, 1)

    a. What is the area of the property?

       A = _____

    b. A site for a house was marked off with vertices at (4, 4), (4, 6), (7, 6), and (7, 4). Find the length and width of the site without graphing the vertices. Check your answer by graphing.

       _____

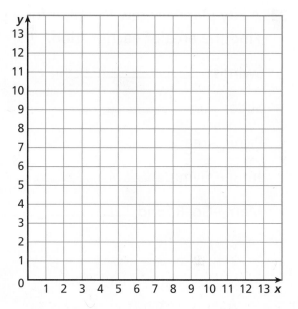

32. An interior designer is tiling a bathroom wall with subway tiles that are 6 units long and 3 units wide. The bottom left corner of the first tile is placed at (0, 0). In the second row of tiles, the bottom left corner of the first whole tile is placed at (3, 3).

    a. How many whole and half tiles will be needed for an 18 by 18 section of the wall?

       _____

    b. Explain how you found the answer.

       _____

       _____

       _____

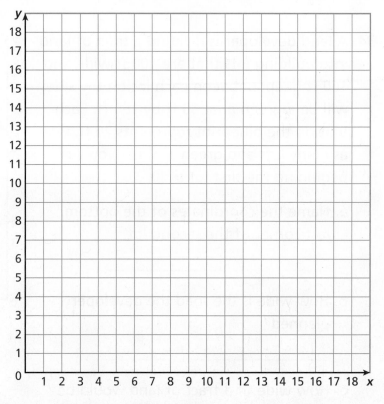

▶ Solve Real World Problems (continued)

33. A city planner drew this plan for a park. Find the area of each section.

Swings: _____

Slide: _____

Picnic Area: _____

Jungle Gym: _____

Merry–Go–Round: _____

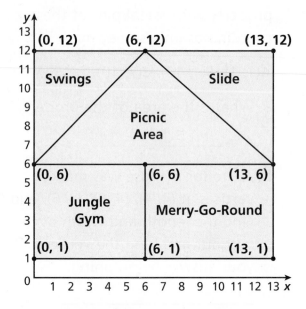

34. A land developer is dividing a tract of land into building lots that are 100 ft wide and 160 ft deep. Between each lot on the sides will be a green area 60 ft by 160 ft. Each unit on the blueprint represents 20 ft. Plot as many lots and green areas as you can beginning the first lot at (0, 3).

a. Name the coordinates of the bottom left corner of the second lot.

_____

b. How wide is the road the developer planned?

_____

c. How wide of a tract of land would be needed for four lots and four green areas?

_____

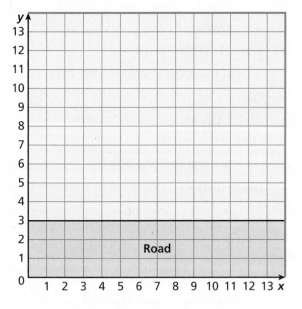

Vocabulary

tessellation

▶ Math and Tiling

In this unit we used squares as standard units of area.
Any figure can be used as a standard unit of area as long
as the figure will cover a surface without gaps or overlaps.
The area of this beehive could be measured in hexagons.

A **tessellation** is a pattern of closed figures that completely
cover a surface with no gaps or overlaps. This beehive is a
tessellation of one figure, a hexagon.

1. Cut out one of these figures from Tessellations (TRB M48).
   Trace it below to show how it can cover a surface
   without gaps or overlaps.

What is the area of your tessellation using the figure
you chose as the unit of area?

▶ Figures That Tessellate

Not all figures can be used as a standard unit of area.

For example, a circle does not **tessellate**, cover a surface without gaps or overlaps.

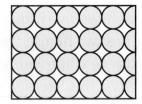

Cut out the figures from Tessellations (TRB 48).
Can each figure be used as a standard unit of area?
If so, draw a tessellation to show how.
Find the area of your tessellations in cm².

2. right triangle

_____

3. regular pentagon

_____

4. trapezoid

_____

5. regular octagon

_____

A tessellation can be made with more than one figure as shown in the pattern of floor tile below.

6. Use a protractor to measure the angles of the figures where their vertices meet at a point. Find the sum of the angles. Do the same for your tessellations above. What can you conclude?

_____

_____

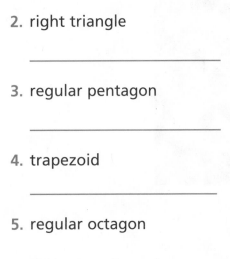

7. Describe how you could find the area covered by the tiles shown in cm²?

_____

_____

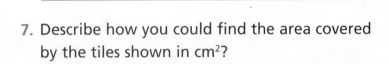

Vocabulary

rhombus
hexagon
octagon
perimeter
area

▶ Vocabulary

Choose the best term from the box.

1. _____ is the amount of surface covered or enclosed by a figure. (Lesson 2-1)

2. A(n) _____ is a polygon with eight sides. (Lesson 2-8)

3. A _____ is a parallelogram with all sides the same length. (Lesson 2-3)

▶ Concepts and Skills

Complete.

4. Why do you use linear units for perimeter and square units for area? (Lesson 2-1)

   _____

   _____

5. What dimensions do you need to find the perimeter and area of the parallelogram at the right? (Lesson 2-5)

   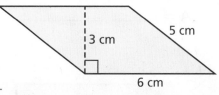
   3 cm   5 cm   6 cm

   Perimeter: _____

   Area: _____

6. Sketch a diagram to show why the area of any triangle is one half the area of its related parallelogram. (Lesson 2-4)

7. Why is decomposing important when finding the area of a complex figure? (Lesson 2-7)

   _____

   _____

8. Why do you subtract the *y*-coordinates, and not the *x*-coordinates, to find the length of a vertical segment on a coordinate grid? (Lesson 2-9)

Find the unknown side length. (Lessons 2-1, 2-2, 2-3, 2-4, 2-5, 2-6, 2-8)

9.
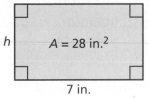

h $A = 28$ in.^{2}

7 in.

$h =$ _____

10.
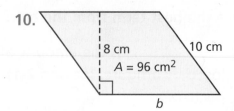

8 cm   10 cm

$A = 96$ cm^2

b

$b =$ _____

Find the perimeter and area of each figure. (Lessons 2-1, 2-2, 2-3, 2-4, 2-5, 2-7)

11.
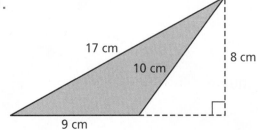

17 cm   8 cm

10 cm

9 cm

$P =$ _____

$A =$ _____

12.
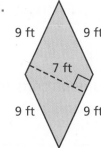

9 ft   9 ft

7 ft

9 ft   9 ft

$P =$ _____

$A =$ _____

13.
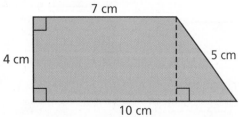

7 cm

4 cm   5 cm

10 cm

$P =$ _____

$A =$ _____

14.
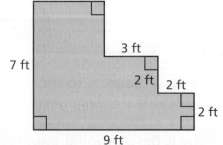

3 ft

7 ft   2 ft   2 ft

2 ft

9 ft

$P =$ _____

$A =$ _____

Name _____   Date _____

Find the perimeter and area of the figure. (Lessons 2-6, 2-7, 2-8)

15.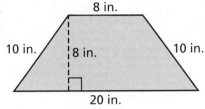

8 in.

10 in.   8 in.   10 in.

20 in.

P = _____

A = _____

16.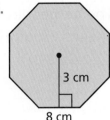

3 cm

8 cm

P = _____

A = _____

Complete. (Lessons 2-4, 2-9)

17. Plot these points on the coordinate grid at the right: A(2, 3), B(11, 7), and C(8, 3). Using a ruler, join the points to form polygon ABC.

18. The length of segment AB is 10 to the nearest unit. The length of segment BC is 5 units. Find the perimeter to the nearest unit and the area of triangle ABC.

    P = _____

    A = _____

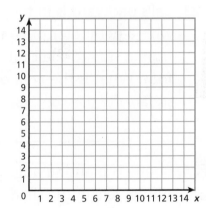

19. What is the length of a segment with these endpoints: (3, 14) and (3, 22)? Is the segment horizontal or vertical?

    _____   _____

▶ Problem Solving

Solve.

20. The floor of Hanh's room is in the shape of a parallelogram that has a base of 4 yards and a height of 3 yards. She wants to cover the floor with carpeting that costs $10 a square yard. How much will the carpeting cost? (Lesson 2-3)

    _____

21. Jamal wants to put a string of lights around a gazebo that is in the shape of a regular hexagon. Each side is 5 ft long. The perpendicular distance to the center is 4 ft to the nearest foot. How many feet of lights will he need? (Lesson 2-8)

_____

22. Casey is making square posters with perimeters of 4 ft. How many square feet of cardboard will Casey need to make 4 posters? (Lesson 2-1)

_____

23. Cal's backyard is in the shape of a regular pentagon with a perimeter of 60 ft. The perpendicular distance from a side to the center is 8 ft to the nearest whole foot. What is the area of his backyard to the nearest square ft? (Lesson 2-8)

_____

Bonne's Flower Garden

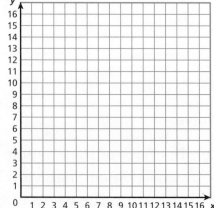

24. Bonne is planting a flower garden. She plans to plant sunflowers in the shaded part of the garden. In how many square feet of the garden will she plant sunflowers? (Lesson 2-2)

_____

25. **Extended Response** A farmer marked the border of a field with posts at these coordinates: D(0, 2), E(6, 10), F(11, 10), and G(16, 2). Each unit represents 1 yd. Describe how to find the area of the field. (Lessons 2-6, 2-9)

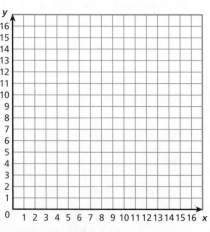

_____

_____

_____

Family Letter

Dear Family,

The goal of this unit of *Math Expressions* is for your child to become fluent with dividing whole numbers and with comparing, adding, subtracting, multiplying, and dividing fractions and decimals. Below is a summary of the topics in this unit.

Addition and Subtraction of Fractions and Decimals

$$\frac{2}{3} + \frac{4}{5} = \frac{10}{15} + \frac{12}{15} = \frac{22}{15} = 1\frac{7}{15}$$

$$\begin{array}{r} \overset{3\ 10}{1.\cancel{40}} \\ -\ 0.25 \\ \hline 1.15 \end{array}$$

Equivalent Fractions

Multiply the numerator and denominator by the same number.	Divide the numerator and denominator by the same number.
$\frac{5}{6} = \frac{5 \bullet 2}{6 \bullet 2} = \frac{10}{12}$	$\frac{10}{12} = \frac{10 \div 2}{12 \div 2} = \frac{5}{6}$

Multiplication of Fractions and Decimals

Multiply numerators and denominators.	Count decimal places in the factors to place the decimal point in the product.
$\frac{2}{3} \bullet \frac{4}{5} = \frac{2 \bullet 4}{3 \bullet 5} = \frac{8}{15}$	$\underset{\text{2 places}}{0.12} \bullet \underset{\text{1 place}}{0.4} = \underset{\text{3 places}}{0.048}$

Division of Fractions and Decimals

Multiply by the reciprocal.	Make the divisor a whole number by multiplying it and the dividend by the same number.
$\frac{2}{5} \div \frac{3}{7} = \frac{2}{5} \bullet \frac{7}{3} = \frac{14}{15}$	
Sometimes you can divide numerators and denominators.	Here we multiply both by 10.
$\frac{8}{15} \div \frac{2}{3} = \frac{8 \div 2}{15 \div 3} = \frac{4}{5}$	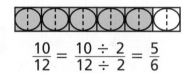

If you have any questions or comments, please call or write to me.

Sincerely,
Your child's teacher

COMMON CORE This unit includes the Common Core Standards for Mathematical Content for The Number System 6.NS.1, 6.NS.2, 6.NS.3, 6.NS.4 and all Mathematical Practices.

Estimada familia,

El objetivo de esta unidad de *Expresiones en matemáticas* es que su hijo domine la división de números enteros y que compare, sume, reste, multiplique y divida correctamente fracciones y decimales. Debajo hay un resumen de algunos de los temas de esta unidad.

Suma y resta de fracciones y decimales

$$\frac{2}{3} + \frac{4}{5} = \frac{10}{15} + \frac{12}{15} = \frac{22}{15} = 1\frac{7}{15}$$

$$\begin{array}{r} {}^{3}\!\!\!\!\!\!\!\!\!\!\!{}^{10} \\ 1.\cancel{40} \\ -\ 0.25 \\ \hline 1.15 \end{array}$$

Fracciones equivalentes

Multiplicar el numerador y el denominador por el mismo número.	Dividir el numerador y el denominador entre el mismo número.

$$\frac{5}{6} = \frac{5 \cdot 2}{6 \cdot 2} = \frac{10}{12}$$

$$\frac{10}{12} = \frac{10 \div 2}{12 \div 2} = \frac{5}{6}$$

Multiplicación de fracciones y decimales

Multiplicar los numeradores y denominadores.

$$\frac{2}{3} \cdot \frac{4}{5} = \frac{2 \cdot 4}{3 \cdot 5} = \frac{8}{15}$$

Contar los lugares decimales en los factores para colocar el punto decimal en la respuesta.

$$0.12 \cdot 0.4 = 0.048$$

$\underset{\text{lugares}}{2} \quad \underset{\text{lugar}}{1} \quad \underset{\text{lugares}}{3}$

División de fracciones y decimales

Multiplicar por el recíproco.

$$\frac{2}{5} \div \frac{3}{7} = \frac{2}{5} \cdot \frac{7}{3} = \frac{14}{15}$$

Algunas veces se pueden dividir los numeradores y denominadores.

$$\frac{8}{15} \div \frac{2}{3} = \frac{8 \div 2}{15 \div 3} = \frac{4}{5}$$

Dividir el divisor y el dividendo entre el mismo número para convertir el divisor en un número entero.

Aquí se multiplican ambos por 10.

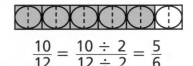

Si tiene preguntas, por favor comuníquese conmigo.

Atentamente,
El maestro de su hijo

© Houghton Mifflin Harcourt Publishing Company. All rights reserved.

Esta unidad incluye los Common Core Standards for Mathematical Content for The Number System 6.NS.1, 6.NS.2, 6.NS.3, 6.NS.4 and all Mathematical Practices.

► Decimal and Whole Number Secret Code Cards

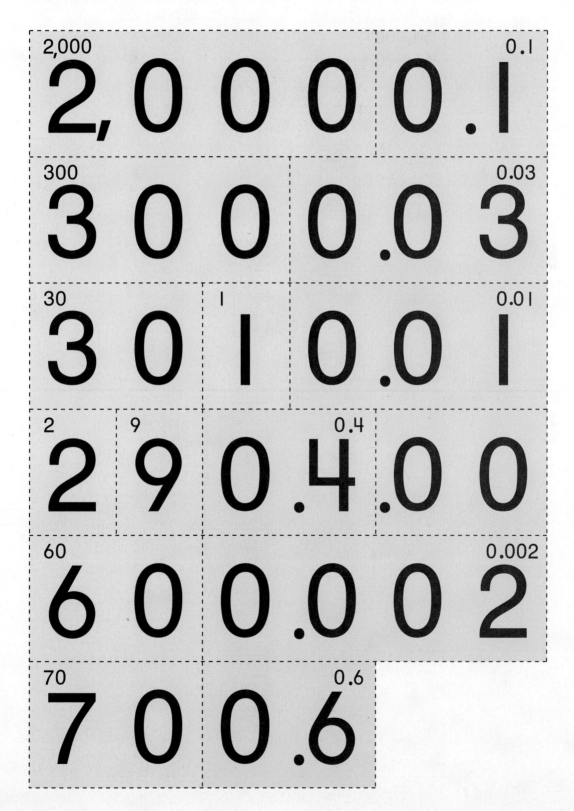

Name _____   **Date** _____

▶ Decimal and Whole Number Secret Code Cards

$1,000
$1,000

$100
$100
$100

$1 $10
$10
$10

$1 $1 $1
$1 $1 $1
$1 $1
$1 $1
$1

$10 $10
$10
$10
$10
$10

$10 $10
$10 $10
$10
$10
$10

Place Value and Whole Number Division

► Discuss and Summarize

Fill in the blanks and discuss how the parts of each problem are related.

Place Value

$\times$ **10** (larger) $\div$ **10** (smaller)

	Thousands	Hundreds	Tens	ONES	Tenths	Hundredths	Thousandths
	1,000.	100.	10.	1.	0.1	0.01	0.001
	$\frac{1000}{1}$	$\frac{100}{1}$	$\frac{10}{1}$	$\frac{1}{1}$	$\frac{1}{10}$	$\frac{1}{100}$	$\frac{1}{1000}$
	$1,000.00	$100.00	$10.00	$1.00	$0.10	$0.01	$0.001
1 a.	2,000 **2,**	300 **3**	60 **6**	**|**	0.6 **.6**	0.03 **3**	0.002 **2**
b.	$1,000 $1,000	$100 $100 $100	$10 $10 $10 $10 $10 $10	$1	(6 coins)	(3 coins)	▷▷

c. $2{,}361.632 = 2{,}000 + \underline{\quad} + \underline{\quad} + \underline{\quad} + \underline{\quad} + \underline{\quad} + 0.002$

					Ones	Tenths	Hundredths	Thousandths
2 a.					0	.6	3	2
b.						$+ \;\overline{\quad 10 \quad}$	$+ \;\overline{\quad 100 \quad}$	$+ \;\overline{\quad 1{,}000 \quad}$
c.						$+ \;\overline{\quad 1{,}000 \quad}$	$+ \;\overline{\quad 1{,}000 \quad}$	$+ \;\overline{\quad 1{,}000 \quad}$
d.					0	.6	0	0
					$+$ 0	.0	3	0
					$+$ 0	.0	0	2
					0	.6	3	2

Vocabulary

dividend
divisor
quotient
remainder

▶ Discuss Division Meanings

The 49 sixth graders raised $2,361 toward their class trip.
How much is that for each student?

When $2,361 is split 49 ways, each student gets $40. Write 4 in the tens place.	Take away the $1,960 that has been shared out, leaving $401 to be shared next.	Each student gets 8 more dollars. Take away the $392 shared out.	There are 9 dollars left, which is 90 dimes. Each student gets 1 dime, so write 1 in the tenths place.
divisor ↓ 4 49)$2,361.00 ↑ **dividend**	4 49)$2,361.00 − 1 96 401	48 49)$2,361.00 − 1 96 401 − 392 9	48.1 49)$2,361.00 − 1 96 401 − 392 9 0
Take away the 49 dimes shared out from the 90 dimes, leaving 41 dimes.	Change the 41 dimes to 410 pennies.	The multiplier 8, which was used before, works again. Each student gets 8 pennies.	That makes 392 pennies shared out of the 410 pennies, leaving 18 pennies.
48.1 49)$2,361.00 1 96 401 − 392 9 0 − 4 9 4 1	48.1 49)$2,361.00 − 1 96 401 − 392 9 0 − 4 9 4 10	48.18 49)$2,361.00 1 96 401 − 392 9 0 − 4 9 4 10	**quotient** → 48.18 49)$2,361.00 − 1 96 401 − 392 9 0 − 4 9 4 10 − 3 92 **remainder** → 18

3. Each student gets $_____ and there are _____ cents left over.

Place Value and Whole Number Division

▶ What's the Error?

Dear Math Students,

I solved the problem 5,619 ÷ 27 on my math homework.
I got 28 R3. I know this can't be right because
27 × 28 is approximately equal to 30 • 30, which is
900. That's not even close to 5,619! Will you look at
my work and help me figure out what I did wrong?

Your friend,
Puzzled Penguin

$$\begin{array}{r} 28 \\ 27\overline{)5,619} \\ \underline{54} \\ 219 \\ \underline{216} \\ 3 \end{array}$$

4. Write an answer to Puzzled Penguin.

_____

_____

_____

_____

_____

_____

▶ Practice Division

Write each answer as a quotient with a remainder.

5. $23\overline{)3,272}$ **6.** $18\overline{)7,342}$ **7.** $19\overline{)3,812}$

Solve.

8. The engineering club won a $1,875 prize in a robot-building
contest. The 16 club members want to share the prize
equally. How much will each member get? How many
cents will be left over?

_____

▶ What's the Error?

Dear Math Students,

I am really having trouble with my math homework today. I had to solve 3,005 ÷ 15. I started, but I got stuck. I know the answer can't be 2, but I don't know what to do next. Can you help me finish the solution?

Your friend,
Puzzled Penguin

$$\begin{array}{r} 2 \\ 15\overline{)3{,}005} \\ \underline{3\,0} \\ 0 \end{array}$$

9. Write an answer to Puzzled Penguin.

_____

_____

_____

_____

_____

_____

▶ Practice Division

Write each answer as a quotient with a remainder.

10. $18\overline{)5{,}402}$

11. $14\overline{)7{,}019}$

12. $33\overline{)2{,}172}$

Solve.

13. Twelve friends earned $4,250 for painting a house. They want to split the money equally. How much will each friend get? How many cents will be left over?

_____

Place Value and Whole Number Division

▶ Adjust the Multiplier by 1

Discuss each step of Nate's and Caity's solutions. Share how you would do that step.

Step 1

Nate	Caity

(90)   6
86) 6,123
    − 5 16
	(90) 7
	86) 6,123
	    − 6 02

Nate Thinks: 7 • 90 = 630, which is more than 612, so 7 is too big for the multiplier. I will use 6. 6 • 6 ones = 36. I write the 6 ones under the 2 and the little 3 tens under the 1, so I remember to add them in. 6 × 8 tens = 48 tens, plus the 3 tens = 51 tens. I cross out the 3 because I already added it. So I get 516.	**Caity Thinks:** 7 • 90 = 630, which is more than 612, but 6 • 90 = 540, which is far from 612. 86 is near the middle between 80 and 90, so I think I will use 7. I know 7 • 6 ones = 42. I write the 2 and remember the 4 tens to add in. 7 times the 8 tens in 86 is 56 tens, plus the 4 tens = 60 tens. So I have 602, which is really 602 tens because the 7 is in the tens place.

Step 2

Nate	Caity

(90)   6
    5 10 12
86) 6,123
    − 5 16
       96
	(90) 7
	86) 6,123
	    − 6 02
	       10

Nate Thinks: I need to ungroup to subtract 516 from 612. I think of 612 as 6 hundreds 1 ten and 2 ones. I ungroup 1 ten and get 10 ones and combine them with the 2 ones to make 12. I need more tens so I ungroup 1 hundred to make 10 tens. Now all the top numbers are greater, so I can subtract. 612 − 516 = 96. I see that 96 is greater than 86. So the multiplier is 7, not 6.	**Caity Writes:** 612 − 602 is 10. The multiplier 7 worked because 10 is less than 86.

▶ **Adjust the Multiplier by 1 (continued)**

Step 3 (Caity has no step to match Nate's Step 3.)

Nate	
$$\begin{array}{r} (90) \quad 7 \\ {\scriptstyle 5\ 10\ 12} \\ 86\overline{)\ 6,1\overset{\scriptstyle 4}{2}3} \\ -\ 6\ 02 \\ \hline 10 \end{array}$$	**Nate Thinks:** 7 • 6 ones is 42, which I write with a little 4 to add in later. 7 • 8 tens = 56 tens, plus the 4 tens I already had, equals 60 tens. So I have 602 (which is really 602 tens because the multiplier 7 is in the tens place). 612 − 602 = 10.

Step 4

Nate	Caity
$$\begin{array}{r} (90) \quad 71 \\ {\scriptstyle 5\ 10\ 12} \\ 86\overline{)\ 6,1\overset{}{2}3} \\ -\ 6\ 02{\scriptstyle 13} \\ \hline \cancel{10}3 \\ -\ 86 \\ \hline 17 \end{array}$$	$$\begin{array}{r} (90) \quad 71 \\ 86\overline{)\ 6,123} \\ -\ 6\ 02 \\ \hline 103 \\ -\ 86 \\ \hline 17 \end{array}$$
Answer: 71 R17	Answer: 71 R17
Nate Thinks: I bring down the 3 to make 103. I can subtract only one group of 86 from 103. I write 1 in the ones place in the quotient. In 103, there are 10 tens, so I regroup 1 ten to make 13 ones. I subtract in each column. 103 − 86 = 17. So, 17 is the remainder.	**Caity Thinks:** I bring down the 3 to make 103. There is just 1 group of 86 in 103. I write 1 in the quotient. Then I subtract 1 • 86 from 103, and the answer is 17. So, the remainder is 17.

1. Write an equation to show Nate and Caity how to check their answers.

_____

Estimated Multipliers in Division

▶ Summarize Multiplying by 0.1 and 0.01

Multiplying by 0.1 is the same as dividing by 10.

$0.1 • 32.4 = 32.4 ÷ 10 = 3.24$

Multiplying a number by 0.1 divides it into 10 parts and takes 1 part. It gives a smaller number. Each digit moves one place right.

You can use this idea to multiply any number of tenths.

Fill in the blanks.

1. a. To find 0.2 • $32.40, divide $32.40 into 10 parts and

    take _____ of those parts.

    $0.2 • \$32.40 = (\$32.40 ÷ 10) •$ _____

   b. To find 6.2 • $32.40, divide $32.40 into _____ parts

    and take _____ of those parts.

    $6.2 • \$32.40 = (\$32.40 ÷$ _____$) •$ _____

Multiplying by 0.01 is the same as dividing by 100.

$0.01 • 32.4 = 32.4 ÷ 100 = 0.324$

Multiplying a number by 0.01 divides it into 100 parts and takes 1 part. It gives an even smaller number. Each digit moves two places right.

You can use this idea to multiply any number of hundredths.

2. a. To find 0.02 • $32.40, divide $32.40 into _____ parts

    and take _____ of those parts.

    $0.02 • \$32.40 = (\$32.40 ÷ 100) •$ _____

   b. To find 0.62 • $32.40, divide $32.40 into _____ parts

    and take _____ of those parts.

    $0.62 • \$32.40 = (\$32.40 ÷$ _____$) •$ _____

▶ Rule About Multiplying Decimals

We can state a rule about multiplying with decimal numbers.

Rule: Ignore the decimal points and multiply. Then place the decimal point so the number of decimal places in the product is equal to the total number of decimal places in the factors.

> **Example**
>
> 0.4 • 0.02
> Ignore decimal point and multiply: 4 • 2 = 8
> Place decimal point so there are three decimal places:
> 0.4 • 0.02 = 0.008
>   1   2   3
> place   places   places

3. Find each product in two ways: 1) Use the rule above; 2) Use the method of dividing into 10 or 100 parts and then multiplying by the number of tenths or hundredths. Show or explain your work. The first one is done for you.

	Use the Rule	Divide into Parts and Multiply
a. 0.2 • 0.3	0.06; two decimal places	(0.3 ÷ 10) • 2 = 0.03 • 2 = 0.06
b. 0.02 • 0.3		
c. 0.2 • 3		
d. 0.02 • 3		
e. 2 • 0.3		
f. 2 • 0.03		

4. Explain why the two methods give the same result.

_____

_____

_____

_____

Use either method to solve these problems.

5. 0.04 • 2 = _____   6. 0.4 • 2 = _____   7. 0.3 • 0.3 = _____   8. 3 • 0.3 = _____

9. 0.04 • 6 = _____   10. 0.5 • 7 = _____   11. 0.3 • 0.8 = _____   12. 7 • 0.6 = _____

Multiplying by a Decimal

▶ Summarize Dividing by 0.1

Dividing by 0.1 gives a number ten times the original number.

$$79.6 \div 0.1 = 10 \cdot 79.6 = 796$$

Dividing by 0.1 is equivalent to multiplying by 10 because there are 10 small parts (tenths) in each whole.

Discuss and explain.

1. Dividing by 0.1 is the same as multiplying by 10.
   Discuss the reason for each numbered step.

$$\frac{79.6}{0.1} \underset{①}{=} \frac{79.6}{0.1} \cdot 1 \underset{②}{=} \frac{79.6}{0.1} \cdot \frac{10}{10} \underset{③}{=} \frac{79.6 \cdot 10}{0.1 \cdot 10} \underset{④}{=} \frac{796}{1} \underset{⑤}{=} 796$$

2. Multiplying a problem in long-division format by
   $1 = \frac{10}{10}$ gives an equivalent problem with a whole
   number divisor.

$$0.1 \overline{)79.6} \longrightarrow 0.1 \overline{)79.6} \qquad OR \qquad 0.1 \overline{)79.6}$$

Complete.

3. The process in Exercise 2 can be used to change *any*
   decimal divisor to a whole number. Use the method
   to rewrite each problem with a whole number divisor.

   a. $0.4 \overline{)2.7}$ b. $72.5 \overline{)0.39}$ c. $2.7 \overline{)9}$ d. $6.3 \overline{)52}$

4. What makes Parts c and d of Exercise 3 trickier than the others?

   _____

   _____

Divide.

5. $0.3 \overline{)9}$ 6. $0.7 \overline{)2.1}$ 7. $1.2 \overline{)480}$ 8. $2.2 \overline{)0.88}$

9. $0.5 \overline{)100}$ 10. $3.2 \overline{)96}$ 11. $0.9 \overline{)10.8}$ 12. $0.8 \overline{)0.64}$

▶ Summarize Dividing by 0.01

Dividing by 0.01 gives a number 100 times the original number.

$$79.6 \div 0.01 = 7{,}960 = 100 \cdot 79.6$$

Dividing by 0.01 is equivalent to multiplying by 100 because there are 100 small parts (hundredths) in each whole.

Discuss and explain.

13. Dividing by 0.01 is the same as multiplying by 100.
    Discuss the reason for each numbered step.

$$\frac{79.6}{0.01} \underset{①}{=} \frac{79.6}{0.01} \cdot 1 \underset{②}{=} \frac{79.6}{0.01} \cdot \frac{100}{100} \underset{③}{=} \frac{79.6 \cdot 100}{0.1 \cdot 100} \underset{④}{=} \frac{7{,}960}{1} \underset{⑤}{=} 7{,}960$$

14. Multiplying a problem in long-division format by
    $1 = \frac{100}{100}$ gives an equivalent problem with a whole
    number divisor.

$$0.01\overline{)79.6} \rightarrow 0.01\overline{)\,79.60\,}^{\bullet} \qquad \text{OR} \qquad 0.01\overline{)\,79.60\,}^{\bullet}$$

Complete.

15. The process in Exercise 14 can be used to change
    any decimal divisor to a whole number. Use the
    method to rewrite each problem with a whole
    number divisor.

   a. $0.04\overline{)2.7}$ b. $7.25\overline{)0.39}$ c. $0.27\overline{)9}$ d. $0.63\overline{)52}$

16. What makes Parts a, c, and d of Exercise 15 tricky?

   _____

   _____

Divide.

17. $0.01\overline{)40}$ 18. $0.03\overline{)0.9}$ 19. $0.12\overline{)48}$ 20. $0.07\overline{)0.49}$

21. $3.21\overline{)6.42}$ 22. $0.25\overline{)7.5}$ 23. $0.11\overline{)990}$ 24. $0.04\overline{)0.16}$

3-5
Class Activity

Name _____

Date _____

▶ Greater, Equal, or Less

1. Explore what happens when you multiply 4 by different numbers.

Case 1: Multiply 4 by a number greater than 1.	**Case 2:** Multiply 4 by 1.	**Case 3:** Multiply 4 by a number less than 1.
$4 \cdot 1.5 =$ _____	$4 \cdot 1 =$ _____	$4 \cdot 0.5 =$ _____
4 units 1.5 units | ? sq. units	4 units 1 unit | ? sq. units	4 units 0.5 units | ? sq. units
Is the product less than, greater than, or equal to 4? _____	Is the product less than, greater than, or equal to 4? _____	Is the product less than, greater than, or equal to 4? _____

2. Multiply 10 by 1, a number greater than 1, and a number less than 1. Tell how each product compares to 10.

_____

_____

3. Explore what happens when you divide 3 by different numbers.

Case 1: Divide 3 by a number greater than 1.	**Case 2:** Divide 3 by 1.	**Case 3:** Divide 3 by a number less than 1.
$3 \div 1.5 =$ _____	$3 \div 1 =$ _____	$3 \div 0.5 =$ _____
? units 1.5 units | 3 sq. units	? units 1 unit | 3 sq. units	? units 0.5 units | 3 sq. units
Is the quotient less than, greater than, or equal to 3? _____	Is the quotient less than, greater than, or equal to 3?	Is the quotient less than, greater than, or equal to 3? _____

4. Divide 12 by 1, a number greater than 1, and a number less than 1. Tell how each quotient compares to 12.

_____

_____

▶ Multiply or Divide

For each problem, decide whether you need to multiply or divide. Then solve.

Show your work.

5. A wallet size photo measures 2.5 inches by 3.5 inches. What is the area of a wallet-size photo?

_____

6. Mr. Diaz paid $5.96 for 4 pounds of broccoli. What was the price per pound?

_____

7. The Washingtons' backyard has an area of 55.48 square meters. If the length of the yard is 7.6 meters, what is the width?

_____

8. In 1976, gas cost about $0.36 per gallon. The gas tank of the car Mr. Renzi drove in that year held 22 gallons. How much did it cost him to fill his gas tank?

_____

9. The area of a king size bed is about 42.2 square feet. A queen size bed is about 0.8 times that size. What is the approximate area of a queen size bed? Round to the nearest tenth of a square foot.

_____

10. A rectangular office has an area of 125 square feet. If the length of the office is 9.5 feet, what is the width? Round to the nearest tenth of a foot.

_____

▶ Greater or Less

Solve.

11. Amber earns $8.50 per hour bagging groceries. Josie, a cashier, earns 1.3 times as much as Amber.

    Does Josie earn more or less than Amber?

    _____

    How much does Josie earn?

    _____

12. On movie night, the student council sold popcorn in 0.75-ounce bags. They sold 180 ounces in all.

    Did they sell more or fewer than 180 bags?

    _____

    How many bags did they sell?

    _____

13. Stickers with the school mascot cost $1.15 each. Manuel bought 9 stickers.

    Did Manuel spend more or less than $9?

    _____

    How much did Manuel spend?

    _____

14. A tabletop is 1.7 meters long and 0.8 meters wide.

    Is the area more or less than 1.7 square meters?

    _____

    What is the area?

    _____

15. Caleb is using thin strips of wood to build a picture frame. One of the strips has a width of 1.2 centimeters and an area of 24.96 square centimeters.

    Is the length of the strip more or less than 24.96 centimeters?

    _____

    What is the length of the strip?

    _____

Name _____   Date _____

▶ Which Is Greater?

Solve without doing any calculations.

16. Which is greater, 18 • 76 or 76 ÷ 18? How do you know?

_____

_____

_____

_____

17. Which is greater, 0.37 • 45 or 45 ÷ 0.37? How do you know?

_____

_____

_____

_____

18. Which is greater, 81 ÷ 12 or 81 ÷ 0.12? How do you know?

_____

_____

_____

_____

19. Which is greater, 23 • 67 or 0.23 • 67? How do you know?

_____

_____

_____

_____

Multiplication or Division

Name _____   Date _____

▶ How Many Decimal Places?

Use the fact that 39 • 74 = 2,886 to solve each problem.

20. 0.39 • 7,400 =   21. 0.39 • 740 =   22. 0.39 • 74 =   23. 39 • 7.4 =

_____   _____   _____   _____

24. 0.74$)\overline{2,886}$ 25. 0.74$)\overline{288.6}$ 26. 0.74$)\overline{28.86}$ 27. 74$)\overline{288.6}$

28. 3.9 • 740 =   29. 3.9 • 74 =   30. 3.9 • 7.4 =   31. 39 • 0.74 =

_____   _____   _____   _____

32. 7.4$)\overline{2,886}$ 33. 7.4$)\overline{288.6}$ 34. 7.4$)\overline{28.86}$ 35. 74$)\overline{28.86}$

Solve.

36. 0.7 • 0.3 = _____   37. 0.06 • 7 = _____   38. 8 • 0.4 = _____

39. 0.12$)\overline{42}$ 40. 3.2$)\overline{2.4}$ 41. 0.06$)\overline{54}$ 42. 0.27$)\overline{1.35}$

43. $\begin{array}{r} 0.09 \\ \times\ \ \ 52 \\ \hline \end{array}$ 44. $\begin{array}{r} 8.5 \\ \times\ 4.2 \\ \hline \end{array}$ 45. $\begin{array}{r} 7.2 \\ \times\ 0.25 \\ \hline \end{array}$ 46. $\begin{array}{r} 18 \\ \times\ 0.6 \\ \hline \end{array}$

47. 3.02$)\overline{90.6}$ 48. 7.5$)\overline{0.06}$ 49. 0.8$)\overline{6.8}$ 50. 0.2$)\overline{0.95}$

▶ How Many Decimal Places? (continued)

Solve.

51. $0.09 \cdot 0.7 = $ _____   52. $50 \cdot 0.5 = $ _____   53. $1.2 \cdot 1.2 = $ _____

54. $0.8\overline{)25.6}$ 55. $0.07\overline{)2.45}$ 56. $1.2\overline{)0.9}$ 57. $0.9\overline{)0.63}$

58. $\begin{array}{r} 0.8 \\ \times\ 6.1 \\ \hline \end{array}$ 59. $\begin{array}{r} 0.33 \\ \times\ \ \ 29 \\ \hline \end{array}$ 60. $\begin{array}{r} 0.46 \\ \times\ \ \ 56 \\ \hline \end{array}$ 61. $\begin{array}{r} 7.5 \\ \times\ 1.9 \\ \hline \end{array}$

62. $2.08\overline{)8.32}$ 63. $0.2\overline{)0.01}$ 64. $0.24\overline{)36}$ 65. $1.2\overline{)1.08}$

▶ The Meaning of the Remainder

Solve.

Show your work.

66. Zola has 575 beads. She needs 32 beads to make a necklace. How many necklaces can she make?

_____

67. At a concert, a band earned $495 for selling 36 CDs. How much did they earn per CD?

_____

68. Mr. Perelli made 500 ounces of raspberry jam. He filled as many 32-ounce jars with jam as he could. How much jam did he have left over?

_____

Multiplication or Division

Name   Date

▶ Comparing Unit Fractions and Decimals

The bar at the top represents a whole watermelon. Below are unit fractions and unit decimals made by dividing the watermelon into equal parts.

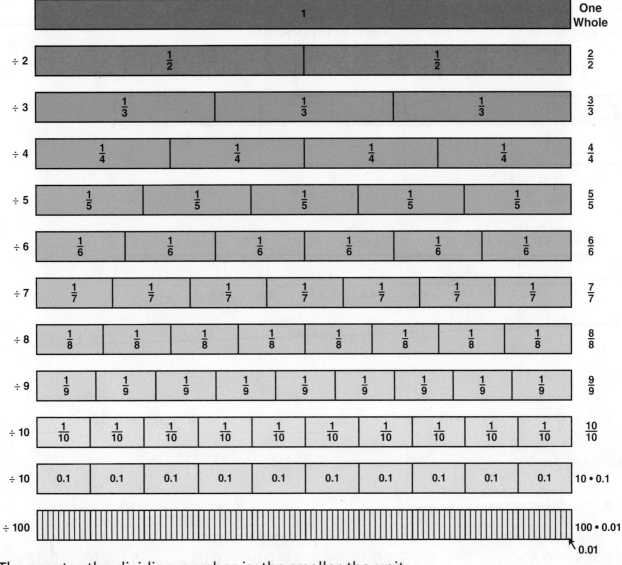

The greater the dividing number is, the smaller the unit fraction or decimal will be. The fraction denominator and the decimal place show the dividing number. So, a greater denominator or decimal place means the whole is divided into smaller parts.

1. 4 > 3, but
$\frac{1}{4}$ ◯ $\frac{1}{3}$

2. 100 > 10, but
0.01 ◯ 0.1

3. 1,000 > 100, but
0.001 ◯ 0.01

Name _____ **Date** _____

Vocabulary

numerator
denominator

▶ Adding and Subtracting Unit Fractions and Decimals

The **denominator** of a fraction tells the number of equal parts the whole is divided into, and, therefore, the number of unit fractions that are made. The **numerator** tells how many of these unit fractions the fraction represents.

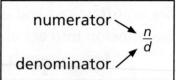

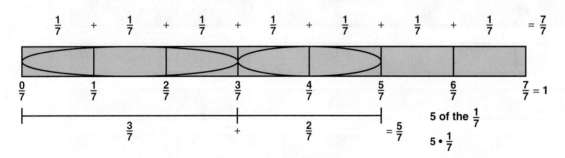

$$\frac{1}{7} + \frac{1}{7} + \frac{1}{7} + \frac{1}{7} + \frac{1}{7} + \frac{1}{7} + \frac{1}{7} = \frac{7}{7}$$

$$\frac{3}{7} + \frac{2}{7} = \frac{5}{7}$$

5 of the $\frac{1}{7}$

$5 \cdot \frac{1}{7}$

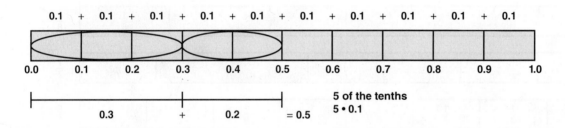

$$0.1 + 0.1 + 0.1 + 0.1 + 0.1 + 0.1 + 0.1 + 0.1 + 0.1 + 0.1$$

$$0.3 + 0.2 = 0.5$$

5 of the tenths
$5 \cdot 0.1$

Add.

4. $\frac{3}{9} + \frac{2}{9} =$ _____

5. $\frac{3}{6} + \frac{2}{6} =$ _____

6. $0.03 + 0.02 =$ _____

Subtract.

7. $\frac{5}{7} - \frac{3}{7} =$ _____

8. $\frac{5}{7} - \frac{2}{7} =$ _____

9. $\frac{5}{9} - \frac{3}{9} =$ _____

10. $\frac{5}{6} - \frac{2}{6} =$ _____

11. $0.5 - 0.3 =$

12. $0.5 - 0.2 =$

13. $0.05 - 0.03 =$

14. $0.05 - 0.02 =$

_____ _____ _____ _____

> To add or subtract fractions with like denominators, add or subtract the numerators.
>
> To add or subtract decimals with like places, add or subtract the numbers in the places.

▶ Discuss Adding and Subtracting Mixed Numbers

Add mixed numbers by adding whole numbers and adding fractions. You may need to make a new group after adding.

Example 1 $1\frac{3}{5} + 2\frac{2}{5}$

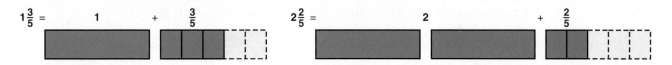

$1\frac{3}{5} =$ 1 $+$ $\frac{3}{5}$ $2\frac{2}{5} =$ 2 $+$ $\frac{2}{5}$

A. $1\frac{3}{5} + 2\frac{2}{5} = 1 + \frac{3}{5} + 2 + \frac{2}{5} = 1 + 2 + \frac{3}{5} + \frac{2}{5} = 3 + \frac{5}{5} = 3 + 1 = 4$

B.
$$
\begin{array}{r}
1\frac{3}{5} \\
+\ 2\frac{2}{5} \\
\hline
3\frac{5}{5} = 3 + 1 = 4
\end{array}
$$

Subtract mixed numbers by ungrouping a 1 if needed.
Then subtract whole numbers and subtract fractions.

Example 2 $2\frac{2}{5} - 1\frac{3}{5}$

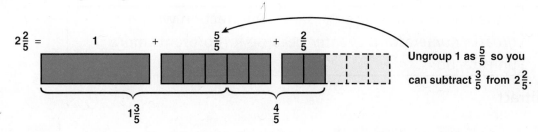

$2\frac{2}{5} =$ 1 $+$ $\frac{5}{5}$ $+$ $\frac{2}{5}$

Ungroup 1 as $\frac{5}{5}$ so you can subtract $\frac{3}{5}$ from $2\frac{2}{5}$.

$1\frac{3}{5}$ $\frac{4}{5}$

Suzy's Method

$\frac{3}{5}$ to $\frac{5}{5}$ is $\frac{2}{5}$ plus $\frac{2}{5} = \frac{4}{5}$.

$2\frac{2}{5} = 1 + \frac{5}{5} + \frac{2}{5}$

$- 1\frac{3}{5} = 1 + \frac{3}{5}$
_____

$\qquad\qquad \frac{2}{5} + \frac{2}{5} = \frac{4}{5}$

Ian's Method

$$
\begin{array}{r}
\overset{\frac{7}{5}}{\cancel{2}\frac{\cancel{2}}{5}} \\
-\ 1\frac{3}{5} \\
\hline
\frac{4}{5}
\end{array}
$$

Youngshim's Method

$2 + \frac{2}{5} = 1 + \frac{7}{5}$

$- 1 + \frac{3}{5} = 1 + \frac{3}{5}$
_____

$0 + \frac{4}{5} = \frac{4}{5}$

3–6
Class Activity

Name _____   Date _____

▶ Practice with Fractions and Decimals

Complete each statement with < or >.

15. $\frac{1}{5}$ ◯ $\frac{1}{4}$ 16. $\frac{1}{8}$ ◯ $\frac{1}{9}$ 17. $\frac{2}{5}$ ◯ $\frac{2}{7}$ 18. 0.6 ◯ 0.06

19. $\frac{3}{5}$ ◯ $\frac{3}{4}$ 20. $\frac{5}{8}$ ◯ $\frac{5}{9}$ 21. $\frac{8}{9}$ ◯ $\frac{8}{10}$ 22. 0.08 ◯ 0.8

> If the numerators are the same, the fraction with the *lesser*
> *denominator* is *greater* because its unit fractions are greater.

Complete each statement with < or >.

23. $2\frac{4}{5}$ ◯ $3\frac{1}{5}$ 24. $6\frac{1}{3}$ ◯ $7\frac{1}{2}$ 25. 2.9 ◯ 3.01   26. $4\frac{3}{7}$ ◯ $4\frac{6}{7}$

> For mixed numbers, if the whole numbers are different, the
> number with the greater whole number is greater. If the
> whole numbers are the same, the number with the greater
> fraction or decimal part is greater.

Complete each statement with < or >.

27. $\frac{5}{8}$ ◯ $\frac{3}{8}$ 28. $\frac{20}{3}$ ◯ $\frac{21}{3}$ 29. 0.4 ◯ 0.5   30. 0.04 ◯ 0.05

> If the denominators are the same, the fraction with the
> *greater numerator* is *greater* because it represents more
> unit fractions.

Add or subtract.

31. $\frac{3}{5} + \frac{4}{5} =$ _____   32. $\frac{7}{8} - \frac{6}{8} =$ _____   33. $3\frac{2}{6} + 4\frac{5}{6} =$ _____

34. $\begin{array}{r} 6.1 \\ -\ 2.2 \\ \hline \end{array}$ 35. $\begin{array}{r} 6\frac{1}{3} \\ -\ 2\frac{2}{3} \\ \hline \end{array}$ 36. $\begin{array}{r} 14.32 \\ -\ 9.56 \\ \hline \end{array}$ 37. $\begin{array}{r} 6\frac{2}{7} \\ -\ 3\frac{5}{7} \\ \hline \end{array}$

38. Jacob used $2\frac{7}{8}$ yards of fabric to make a banner. He
added another $\frac{5}{8}$ yard of fabric to decorate the banner.
How much fabric did he use?

_____

Comparing, Adding, and Subtracting with the Same Unit

Vocabulary

equivalent fractions

▶ What Are Equivalent Fractions?

Each fraction bar shows a fraction equivalent to $\frac{5}{6}$.

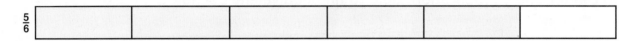

A. Split each sixth into two equal parts to make 10 twelfths.

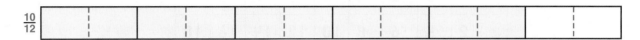

Numerically: $\frac{5 \cdot 2}{6 \cdot 2} = \frac{10}{12}$. We have more, but smaller, parts.

B. Split each sixth into three equal parts to make 15 eighteenths.

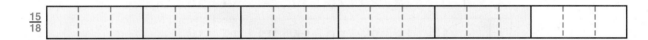

Numerically: $\frac{5 \cdot 3}{6 \cdot 3} = \frac{15}{18}$. We have more, but smaller, parts.

C. Split each sixth into four equal parts to make 20 twenty-fourths.

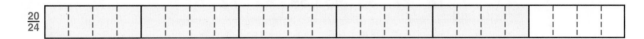

Numerically: $\frac{5 \cdot 4}{6 \cdot 4} = \frac{20}{24}$. We have more, but smaller, parts.

You can make equivalent fractions by

▶ Multiplying to make more, but smaller, parts, as in the examples above.

▶ Dividing to make fewer, but larger, parts.

For example, to simplify $\frac{10}{12}$, form groups of two twelfths to get 5 sixths.

Numerically: $\frac{10 \div 2}{12 \div 2} = \frac{5}{6}$ Think: $\frac{2}{2} \cdot \boxed{\frac{5}{6}} = \frac{10}{12}$

Name _____   Date _____

▶ Seeing Equivalent Fractions in the Multiplication Table

You can use the multiplication table to find equivalent fractions.

•	1	2	3	4	5	6	7	8	9
1	1	2	3	4	5	6	7	8	9
2	2	4	6	8	10	12	14	16	18
3	3	6	9	12	15	18	21	24	27
4	4	8	12	16	20	24	28	32	36
5	5	10	15	20	25	30	35	40	45
6	6	12	18	24	30	36	42	48	54
7	7	14	21	28	35	42	49	56	63
8	8	16	24	32	40	48	56	64	72
9	9	18	27	36	45	54	63	72	81

$$\quad\quad\quad\quad \cdot 2 \quad \cdot 3 \quad \cdot 4 \quad \cdot 5 \quad \cdot 6 \quad \cdot 7 \quad \cdot 8 \quad \cdot 9$$

$$\frac{5}{6} \quad \frac{10}{12} \quad \frac{15}{18} \quad \frac{20}{24} \quad \frac{25}{30} \quad \frac{30}{36} \quad \frac{35}{42} \quad \frac{40}{48} \quad \frac{45}{54}$$

$$\quad\quad\quad\quad \cdot 2 \quad \cdot 3 \quad \cdot 4 \quad \cdot 5 \quad \cdot 6 \quad \cdot 7 \quad \cdot 8 \quad \cdot 9$$

Use the multiplication table to write fractions equivalent to the given fraction.

1. $\dfrac{3}{5} =$ _____ $=$ _____ $=$ _____ $=$ _____ $=$ _____ $=$ _____ $=$ _____

2. $\dfrac{4}{7} =$ _____ $=$ _____ $=$ _____ $=$ _____ $=$ _____ $=$ _____ $=$ _____

Equivalent Fractions or Decimals

▶ Finding a Common Denominator

Example 1 $\frac{4}{5} + \frac{3}{10}$

Jo Anne's Solution

I look at the denominators to see what I need to multiply by.

$\frac{4}{5} + \frac{3}{10} = \frac{4 \cdot 2}{5 \cdot 2} + \frac{3}{10} = \frac{8}{10} + \frac{3}{10} = \frac{11}{10} = 1\frac{1}{10}$

$\cdot 2$

Mark's Solution

I see $5 \cdot 2 = 10$.	So, I multiply 4 and 5 by 2.	I find how many tenths.	Now I can add.
$\frac{4 \cdot}{5 \cdot 2} = \frac{}{10}$	$\frac{4 \cdot 2}{5 \cdot 2} = \frac{}{10}$	$\frac{4 \cdot 2}{5 \cdot 2} = \frac{8}{10}$	$\frac{4}{5} + \frac{3}{10} = \frac{8}{10} + \frac{3}{10}$
			$= \frac{11}{10} = 1\frac{1}{10}$

> To compare, add, or subtract two fractions when the denominator of one is a factor of the denominator of the other, change the fraction with the lesser denominator to an equivalent fraction that uses the greater denominator.

Example 2 $0.2 + 0.03$

Shauna's Solution

0.2 is two dimes. That is 20 pennies, so $0.2 = 0.20$.
I add like places.

$$\begin{array}{r} 0.20 \\ + 0.03 \\ \hline 0.23 \end{array}$$

> To compare, add, or subtract decimals with different numbers of places, put zeros on the end of the decimal with fewer places to make the number of decimal places in the two numbers equal.

Compare, add, or subtract.

3. $0.07 \bigcirc 0.4$ 4. $0.1 \bigcirc 0.06$ 5. $\frac{2}{5} \bigcirc \frac{8}{15}$ 6. $\frac{3}{4} \bigcirc \frac{8}{12}$

7. $\frac{5}{6} - \frac{11}{24} =$ _____   8. $0.4 - 0.08 =$ _____

9. $0.3 - 0.02 =$ _____   10. $\frac{4}{5} + \frac{17}{30} =$ _____

▶ What's the Error?

Dear Math Students,

My friend Wendy had a pizza party. After the party, she had $\frac{1}{3}$ of a cheese pizza left. She also had $\frac{1}{6}$ of a pepperoni pizza. I told Wendy that together she has $\frac{2}{9}$ of a whole pizza left. She says that can't be right.

Can you help me figure out my mistake? How much of a whole pizza does Wendy have?

Your friend,

Puzzled Penguin

11. Write an answer to Puzzled Penguin.

_____

_____

_____

_____

Name _____   Date _____

Vocabulary

common factor
common denominator

▶ Common Denominators for Other Cases

Case 1: Denominators with no common factor except 1

$\frac{2}{3} + \frac{5}{4}$

Virginia's Solution: I need to find a common denominator. 3 • 4 is 12. So, if I multiply the numerator and denominator of each fraction by the other factor, they'll both have the denominator 12.

$$\frac{2 \cdot 4}{3 \cdot 4} + \frac{5 \cdot 3}{4 \cdot 3} = \frac{8}{12} + \frac{15}{12}$$
$$= \frac{23}{12} = 1\frac{11}{12}$$

Add or subtract.

1. $\frac{4}{5} + \frac{2}{3} =$ _____

2. $\frac{3}{5} - \frac{1}{6} =$ _____

Case 2: Denominators with a common factor that is not one of the numbers

$\frac{3}{4} + \frac{5}{6}$

Roger's Solution: I think of a number that is a multiple of both denominators. 12 is a multiple of 4 and 6. Then I think of what to multiply the denominator of each fraction by to get 12. I multiply the numerator and denominator by that number.

$$\frac{3}{4} + \frac{5}{6} = \frac{3 \cdot 3}{4 \cdot 3} + \frac{5 \cdot 2}{6 \cdot 2}$$
$$= \frac{9}{12} + \frac{10}{12}$$
$$= \frac{19}{12} = 1\frac{7}{12}$$

Serena's Solution: If I can't think of a common multiple, I just use Virginia's method and multiply the numerator and denominator of each fraction by the other factor.

$$\frac{3}{4} + \frac{5}{6} = \frac{18}{24} + \frac{20}{24}$$
$$= \frac{38}{24} = 1\frac{14}{24} = 1\frac{7}{12}$$

Add or subtract.

3. $\frac{5}{6} + \frac{3}{8} =$ _____

4. $\frac{5}{9} - \frac{1}{6} =$ _____

▶ Practice With Common Denominators

Complete each statement with < or >.

5. $\dfrac{5}{6} \bigcirc \dfrac{7}{9}$

6. $\dfrac{5}{8} \bigcirc \dfrac{4}{6}$

7. $\dfrac{5}{7} \bigcirc \dfrac{3}{4}$

8. $\dfrac{3}{5} \bigcirc \dfrac{2}{3}$

Add or subtract.

9. $\dfrac{5}{6} + \dfrac{1}{4} =$ _____

10. $\dfrac{2}{5} + \dfrac{4}{7} =$ _____

11. $3\dfrac{4}{5} + 6\dfrac{2}{3} =$ _____

12. $4\dfrac{1}{2} + 2\dfrac{5}{9} =$ _____

13. $6\dfrac{7}{10} - 5\dfrac{7}{8} =$ _____

14. $3\dfrac{4}{5} - 1\dfrac{5}{6} =$ _____

15. $7\dfrac{2}{3} - 1\dfrac{3}{4} =$ _____

16. $6\dfrac{4}{7} - 2\dfrac{2}{3} =$ _____

17. A recipe calls for $\dfrac{1}{3}$ cup of flour. Another recipe calls for $\dfrac{3}{4}$ cup of flour. How much flour do you need to make both recipes? _____

Finding a Common Unit Fraction

Vocabulary

least common multiple

▶ Strategies for Common Denominators

1. The denominators of several pairs of fractions are shown below.

    4, 8   4, 3   4, 6   5, 10   5, 7   8, 12   6, 8   6, 12   6, 7

    List each pair of denominators beside the case that best describes it.
    Think about the strategy you would use to find a common
    denominator for the pair

    Case A One denominator is a factor of the other.   _____

    Case B The denominators have no common factors
    other than 1.   _____

    Case C The denominators have a common factor that
    is not one of the numbers and is not 1.   _____

▶ Least Common Multiple

2. The **least common multiple (LCM)** of two numbers is
    the least number that is a multiple of both numbers.
    Find the LCM of each pair of numbers.

    a. 4, 6 _____   b. 4, 10 _____   c. 6, 8 _____   d. 6, 9 _____

    e. 6, 10 _____   f. 8, 10 _____   g. 8, 12 _____   h. 9, 12 _____

    i. 10, 12 _____   j. 4, 8 _____   k. 3, 9 _____   l. 5, 9 _____

3. Pairs a through i represent which case? What strategy
    can you use to find the LCM?

    _____

4. Pairs j and k represent which case? How do you know
    the answer you found is the LCM?

    _____

5. Pair l represents which case? How do you know
    the answer you found is the LCM?

    _____

> The LCM can be one of the denominators (Case A) or
> the product of the denominators (Case B) or a multiple
> of both denominators (Case C). We can always use the
> product of the denominators as a common denominator.

▶ Solve Real World Problems

Write an equation and use it to solve the problem.

Show your work.

6. In a frog-hopping contest, the frog that hops farthest in two hops wins. On the second hop, your frog hops $\frac{3}{8}$ yard. He hopped a total of $\frac{15}{16}$ yard. How long was his first hop?

_____

7. The planning committee for a class party bought 6.5 liters of juice. After the party, they had 2.75 liters left. How much juice did the class drink at the party?

_____

8. Diana and James are painting a room together. Diana paints $\frac{1}{3}$ of the room and James paints $\frac{1}{4}$ of the room. How much of the room have they painted?

_____

9. A carpenter cuts a piece 0.75 meters long from a board. The remaining board is 1.5 meters long. How long was the board before the carpenter cut it?

_____

10. A teacher brought some colored beads to class. During class, her students used $1\frac{2}{9}$ bags of beads. The teacher was left with $1\frac{5}{6}$ bags. How many bags of beads did she bring to class?

_____

11. Pedro wrote a math riddle for his friends.
    Guess my number, I'll tell you more:
    Subtract me from $6\frac{5}{8}$, and you'll get four!
    What is Pedro's number?

_____

Mixed Problem Solving

Name   Date

▶ Mixed Practice

Add.

12. $0.04 + 0.1 =$ _____

13. $\frac{2}{3} + 1\frac{2}{9} =$ _____

14. $\frac{3}{7} + \frac{1}{7} =$ _____

15. $\frac{1}{5} + \frac{1}{6} =$ _____

16. $1.2 + 2.03 =$ _____

17. $4\frac{5}{9} + 1\frac{5}{6} =$ _____

18. $2\frac{3}{10} + 3\frac{1}{4} =$ _____

19. $5.2 + 2.15 =$ _____

Subtract.

20. $\frac{2}{3} - \frac{1}{4} =$ _____

21. $1.4 - 0.25 =$ _____

22. $4\frac{2}{5} - 1\frac{3}{10} =$ _____

23. $1\frac{5}{6} - \frac{1}{3} =$ _____

24. $1.37 - 0.4 =$ _____

25. $3\frac{3}{10} - 2\frac{5}{8} =$ _____

26. $\frac{8}{11} - \frac{1}{3} =$ _____

27. $5.6 - 3.04 =$ _____

Name _____ **Date** _____

▶ Strategies for Comparing

Look for patterns in the fractions and decimals below.

$1 = \frac{2}{2} = \frac{4}{4} = \frac{8}{8}$ —— $1.000 = 1.0$

$\frac{7}{8}$ —— 0.9 / 0.875

$0.83 \approx \frac{5}{6}$
$0.8 = \frac{4}{5}$

$\frac{3}{4} = \frac{6}{8}$ —— $0.750 = 0.75$

0.7
$0.67 \approx \frac{4}{6} = \frac{2}{3}$

$\frac{5}{8}$ —— 0.625
$0.6 = \frac{3}{5}$

$\frac{1}{2} = \frac{2}{4} = \frac{4}{8}$ —— $0.500 = 0.50$
$= 0.5 = \frac{3}{6}$

$0.4 = \frac{2}{5}$
$\frac{3}{8}$ —— 0.375

$0.33 \approx \frac{2}{6} = \frac{1}{3}$
0.3

$\frac{1}{4} = \frac{2}{8}$ —— $0.250 = 0.25$
$0.2 = \frac{1}{5}$
$0.17 \approx \frac{1}{6}$
$\frac{1}{8}$ —— 0.125
0.1

$\frac{0}{2} = \frac{0}{4} = \frac{0}{8}$ —— 0.000

Below are general and special cases for comparing fractions and decimals.

General Cases

Case 1: Same denominator or number of places
Fraction with greater numerator is greater.
Ignore decimal point. Greater number is greater.

$\frac{3}{5} \bigcirc \frac{4}{5}$

$0.7 > 0.5$

Case 2: Same numerator or digits
Fraction with lesser denominator is greater.
Decimal with leftmost non-zero digit is greater.

$\frac{6}{9} \bigcirc \frac{6}{8}$

$0.3 \bigcirc 0.03$

Case 3: Different denominators
Find equivalent fractions with a common denominator to change fractions to Case 1.

$\frac{3}{4} \bigcirc \frac{2}{3}$

Case 4: Mixed numbers
Number with greater whole number is greater. If whole numbers are the same, compare fractions using Cases 1–3.

$5\frac{1}{8} \bigcirc 2\frac{9}{10}$

$4.7 > 4.07$

Special Cases for Fractions

Case 5: Denominators are factors of 10 or 100.
Compare the decimal equivalents.

$\frac{3}{5} \bigcirc \frac{4}{10}$

Case 6: One fraction $> \frac{1}{2}$. One fraction $< \frac{1}{2}$.
Fraction $> \frac{1}{2}$ is greater.

$\frac{5}{8} \bigcirc \frac{3}{7}$

Use strategies to compare.

28. $0.76 \bigcirc 0.67$ 29. $\frac{2}{3} \bigcirc \frac{7}{12}$ 30. $1\frac{1}{2} \bigcirc 1\frac{2}{5}$

31. $\frac{5}{8} \bigcirc \frac{5}{6}$ 32. $0.09 \bigcirc 0.1$ 33. $\frac{4}{9} \bigcirc \frac{3}{5}$

Mixed Problem Solving

▶ Multiplying by Fractions and Decimals Less than 1

Example 1

A. $0.1 \cdot 4 = 0.1(1 + 1 + 1 + 1) = 0.1 + 0.1 + 0.1 + 0.1 = 0.4 = 4 \div 10$

$\frac{1}{10} \cdot 4 = \frac{1}{10}(1 + 1 + 1 + 1) = \frac{1}{10} + \frac{1}{10} + \frac{1}{10} + \frac{1}{10} = \frac{4}{10} = 4 \div 10$

B. $0.2 \cdot 4 = 2 \cdot 0.1 \cdot 4 = 2 \cdot 0.4 = 0.8$ So, $0.2 \cdot 4 = (4 \div 10) \cdot 2$.

$\frac{2}{10} \cdot 4 = 2 \cdot \frac{1}{10} \cdot 4 = 2 \cdot \frac{4}{10} = \frac{8}{10}$ So, $\frac{2}{10} \cdot 4 = (4 \div 10) \cdot 2$.

Example 2

Remember, any whole number can be written as a fraction that has a denominator of 1. So, $4 = \frac{4}{1}$ and $w = \frac{w}{1}$.

A. $\frac{1}{d} \cdot w = \frac{1 \cdot w}{d \cdot 1} = w \div d = \frac{w}{d}$

$\frac{1}{3} \cdot 4 = \frac{1 \cdot 4}{3 \cdot 1} = 4 \div 3 = \frac{4}{3}$

$\frac{1}{3}$ of 4 rectangles is $\frac{1}{3} + \frac{1}{3} + \frac{1}{3} + \frac{1}{3} = \frac{4}{3}$.

B. $\frac{n}{d} \cdot w = \frac{n \cdot w}{d \cdot 1} = \frac{n \cdot w}{d}$

$\frac{2}{3} \cdot 4 = \frac{2 \cdot 4}{3 \cdot 1} = 8 \div 3 = \frac{8}{3}$

$\frac{2}{3}$ of 4 rectangles is $\frac{2}{3} + \frac{2}{3} + \frac{2}{3} + \frac{2}{3} = \frac{8}{3}$.

C. $w \cdot \frac{n}{d} = \frac{w \cdot n}{1 \cdot d} = \frac{w \cdot n}{d}$

$4 \cdot \frac{2}{3} = \frac{4 \cdot 2}{3} = \frac{8}{3}$

4 groups of $\frac{2}{3}$ is $\frac{2}{3} + \frac{2}{3} + \frac{2}{3} + \frac{2}{3} = \frac{8}{3}$.

> Multiplying a number *n* by a fraction less than 1 produces a product less than *n* because only part of *n* is being taken.

Name _____   Date _____

▶ Multiplying Fractions

Example

$$\frac{a}{b} \cdot \frac{c}{d} = \frac{a \cdot c}{b \cdot d} \qquad \frac{2}{3} \cdot \frac{4}{5} = \frac{2 \cdot 4}{3 \cdot 5} = \frac{8}{15}$$

Here are two different ways to model the product of $\frac{2}{3}$ and $\frac{4}{5}$.

Ginny's Model "I use a number line. First I model $\frac{4}{5}$ (red loop), and then I separate each fifth into 3 equal parts, or thirds (green tick marks). This makes 15 equal parts altogether. Then I take $\frac{2}{3}$ of each fifth (blue loops), which is $\frac{8}{15}$."

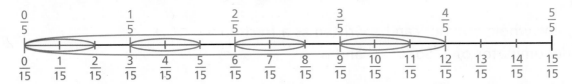

Taylor's Model "I use an area model. First, I model $\frac{4}{5}$ by dividing the area of a square into fifths and shading 4 of them red. To find $\frac{2}{3}$ of those 4 fifths, I divide the area into thirds and shade 2 of them blue. The whole area is divided into fifteenths, and there are 8 fifteenths in which the shading overlaps."

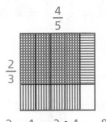

$$\frac{2}{3} \cdot \frac{4}{5} = \frac{2 \cdot 4}{3 \cdot 5} = \frac{8}{15}$$

1. Explain how the model at the right shows $\frac{7}{3} \cdot \frac{4}{5}$.

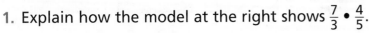

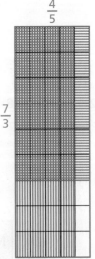

$$\frac{7}{3} \cdot \frac{4}{5} = \frac{7 \cdot 4}{3 \cdot 5} = \frac{28}{15} = 1\frac{13}{15}$$

▶ Multiplying in Different Cases

Multiply.

2. $\frac{5}{8} \cdot 9 =$ _____

3. $\frac{3}{4} \cdot 6 =$ _____

4. $\frac{2}{5} \cdot 10 =$ _____

5. $12 \cdot \frac{5}{6} =$ _____

6. $4 \cdot \frac{2}{7} =$ _____

7. $7 \cdot \frac{4}{9} =$ _____

8. $\frac{3}{5} \cdot \frac{5}{9} =$ _____

9. $\frac{5}{6} \cdot \frac{1}{3} =$ _____

10. $\frac{3}{7} \cdot \frac{1}{8} =$ _____

11. $\frac{1}{2} \cdot \frac{1}{5} =$ _____

12. $\frac{3}{8} \cdot \frac{2}{6} =$ _____

13. $\frac{4}{9} \cdot \frac{5}{7} =$ _____

14. $2\frac{3}{5} \cdot 4\frac{2}{3} =$ _____

15. $3\frac{1}{3} \cdot 4\frac{2}{5} =$ _____

16. $1\frac{2}{7} \cdot 2\frac{3}{8} =$ _____

17. Judy has a $\frac{4}{5}$-liter bottle of juice. Fuchang's bottle of juice contains $\frac{2}{3}$ as much as Judy's bottle.

   a. Does Fuchang have more or less juice than Judy? How do you know?

   _____

   b. How much juice does he have? Which operation did you use?

   _____

   c. How much more or less juice does he have? Which operation did you use to decide?

   _____

▶ What's the Error?

Dear Math Students,

I am going to make turkey burgers for a barbecue. I'll use $\frac{1}{4}$ pound of turkey for each burger. Since I want to make 6 burgers, I'll need to buy $\frac{1}{24}$ pound of turkey. Does that sound reasonable? Or what mistake did I make?

Your friend,
Puzzled Penguin

18. Write a response to Puzzled Penguin.

_____

_____

_____

Dear Math Students,

I am planting a flower garden! The space I have to plant in is $3\frac{1}{2}$ feet wide and $4\frac{1}{2}$ feet long. I told my friend that the area of my flower garden is $12\frac{1}{4}$ square feet. She says I've made a mistake! Can you help me find my mistake, and the correct area?

Your friend,
Puzzled Penguin

19. Write a response to Puzzled Penguin.

_____

_____

_____

Multiplying with Fractions

▶ Divide with Unit Fractions

Complete the statements.

1. Three friends divide 2 submarine sandwiches equally. What part of a sandwich does each friend receive?

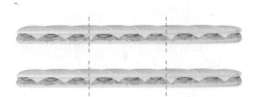

$2 \div 3 = \frac{1}{3} \cdot 2 = \frac{1}{3}(1 + 1) = \frac{1}{3} + \frac{1}{3} = $ _____

Each friend receives _____ of a sandwich.

2. If the three friends divide 5 sandwiches equally, what part of a sandwich will each friend receive?

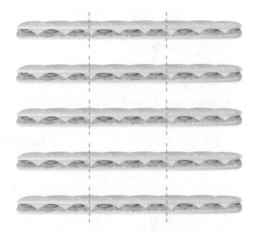

$5 \div 3 = \frac{1}{3} \cdot 5 = \frac{1}{3}(1 + 1 + 1 + 1 + 1)$

$= \frac{1}{3} + \frac{1}{3} + \frac{1}{3} + \frac{1}{3} + \frac{1}{3} = $ _____

Each friend receives _____ sandwiches.

3. Sasha has $\frac{1}{3}$ of a sandwich. He divides it into 2 equal parts and gives one part to his sister. What part of a sandwich does his sister receive?

$\frac{1}{3} \div 2 = \frac{1}{3} \cdot \frac{1}{2} = $ _____

His sister receives _____ of a sandwich.

4. If Sasha divided the $\frac{1}{3}$ of a sandwich into 5 equal parts, what part of a sandwich would each part represent?

$\frac{1}{3} \div 5 = \frac{1}{3} \cdot \frac{1}{5} = $ _____

Each part would represent _____ of a sandwich.

▶ Divide with Unit Fractions (continued)

5. How many $\frac{1}{3}$ sandwiches are in 2 sandwiches?

$2 \div \frac{1}{3} = 2 \cdot 3 = $ _____

There are three $\frac{1}{3}$ sandwiches in *each* sandwich because $1 = \frac{3}{3}$.

So, there are _____ $\frac{1}{3}$ sandwiches altogether.

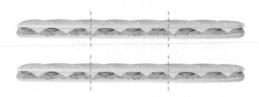

6. How many $\frac{1}{3}$ sandwiches are in 5 sandwiches?

$5 \div \frac{1}{3} = 5 \cdot 3 = $ _____

There are three $\frac{1}{3}$ sandwiches in each sandwich because $1 = \frac{3}{3}$.

So, there are _____ $\frac{1}{3}$ sandwiches altogether.

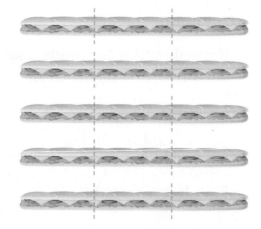

You just explored three cases of division:

Case 1: If w and d are whole numbers, then
$$w \div d = w \cdot \frac{1}{d}.$$

Case 2: If w is a whole number and $\frac{1}{d}$ is a unit fraction, then $\frac{1}{d} \div w = \frac{1}{d} \cdot \frac{1}{w}.$

Case 3: If w is a whole number and $\frac{1}{d}$ is a unit fraction, then $w \div \frac{1}{d} = w \cdot d.$

The **reciprocal** of a fraction $\frac{a}{b}$ is $\frac{b}{a}$. (So, the reciprocal of whole number w, or $\frac{w}{1}$, is $\frac{1}{w}$.)

> To divide a unit fraction by a whole number or a whole number by a unit fraction, multiply by the reciprocal of the divisor.

▶ Divide with Unit Fractions (continued)

Write the reciprocal of the divisor to make each statement true.

7. $3 \div 4 = 3 \cdot$ _____

8. $10 \div 2 = 10 \cdot$ _____

9. $\frac{1}{6} \div 5 = \frac{1}{6} \cdot$ _____

10. $\frac{1}{3} \div 8 = \frac{1}{3} \cdot$ _____

11. $4 \div \frac{1}{9} = 4 \cdot$ _____

12. $7 \div \frac{1}{2} = 7 \cdot$ _____

▶ Divide in Different Cases

Divide. Look at the Fraction Poster for help.

13. $5 \div 7 =$ _____

14. $\frac{1}{4} \div 2 =$ _____

15. $8 \div \frac{1}{2} =$ _____

16. $\frac{1}{3} \div 6 =$ _____

17. $9 \div 10 =$ _____

18. $7 \div \frac{1}{9} =$ _____

19. $12 \div \frac{1}{4} =$ _____

20. $\frac{1}{5} \div 5 =$ _____

21. $6 \div 11 =$ _____

22. $\frac{1}{8} \div 12 =$ _____

23. $3 \div 2 =$ _____

24. $9 \div \frac{1}{5} =$ _____

25. $7 \div 3 =$ _____

26. $8 \div \frac{1}{6} =$ _____

27. $\frac{1}{3} \div 9 =$ _____

28. $1 \div 8 =$ _____

29. $\frac{1}{6} \div 3 =$ _____

30. $16 \div 4 =$ _____

31. $\frac{1}{4} \div 11 =$ _____

32. $2 \div \frac{1}{5} =$ _____

33. $6 \div \frac{1}{2} =$ _____

▶ Solve Word Problems

34. Greenie the grasshopper hopped 3 meters in the length of time it took Tiny the ant to crawl $\frac{1}{5}$ meter. Greenie hopped how many times as far as Tiny crawled? Explain your answer.

_____

_____

_____

35. Tiny crawled how many times as far as Greenie hopped? Explain your answer.

_____

_____

_____

▶ What's the Error?

Dear Math Students,

The problem below was marked wrong on my math quiz.

$$\frac{1}{3} \div 4 = \frac{3}{1} \cdot 4 = \frac{3}{1} \cdot \frac{4}{1} = \frac{12}{1} = 12$$

Can you describe my mistake and explain how I can find the correct quotient? Thank you.

Your friend,
Puzzled Penguin

36. _____

_____

_____

Dividing with Fractions and Whole Numbers

▶ Is it Multiplication or Division?

Name the operation needed to solve the problem, and predict the size of the result. Then solve.

1. Sujita makes 6 quarts of lemonade to sell at her lemonade stand. Her friend Tess makes $\frac{2}{3}$ as much lemonade. Does Tess make more or less lemonade than Sujita?

   _____

   _____

   Find the amount of lemonade Tess makes. _____

2. A tractor loader has a capacity of $\frac{1}{7}$ ton, and will be used to move 2 tons of topsoil. Will the loader be filled fewer or more than 2 times?

   _____

   _____

   How many times will the loader be filled? _____

3. An artist can paint 3 decorative boxes per hour. One day, she painted for $\frac{1}{2}$ hour. Did she paint more or fewer than 3 boxes?

   _____

   _____

   Find the number of boxes the artist painted. _____

4. Anthony rides his bike 2 miles. Stephen rides his bike $\frac{1}{3}$ mile. Does Anthony ride more or less than twice as far as Stephen?

   _____

   _____

   Find how many times as far Anthony rides. _____

▶ Greater Than or Less Than?

> Multiplying by a fraction less than 1 gives a lesser answer.
> Dividing by a fraction less than 1 gives a greater answer.

Multiply or divide.

5. $8 \div 10 =$ _____

6. $4 \cdot \frac{1}{2} =$ _____

7. $\frac{2}{3} \cdot \frac{1}{6} =$ _____

8. $\frac{3}{4} \cdot \frac{3}{4} =$ _____

9. $5 \div \frac{1}{3} =$ _____

10. $\frac{1}{4} \div 7 =$ _____

11. $\frac{5}{3} \cdot \frac{3}{6} =$ _____

12. $7 \div 3 =$ _____

13. $10 \div \frac{1}{5} =$ _____

14. $\frac{5}{8} \cdot \frac{2}{3} =$ _____

15. $\frac{3}{4} \cdot \frac{2}{6} =$ _____

16. $\frac{1}{3} \div 10 =$ _____

17. $3\frac{1}{2} \cdot 5 =$ _____

18. $4 \cdot 1\frac{2}{3} =$ _____

19. $5 \div 4 =$ _____

20. $6 \div \frac{1}{9} =$ _____

21. $3\frac{5}{8} \cdot 2\frac{1}{3} =$ _____

22. $1\frac{2}{5} \cdot 3\frac{1}{3} =$ _____

23. $8 \div 11 =$ _____

24. $\frac{1}{3} \div 6 =$ _____

25. $12 \div \frac{1}{4} =$ _____

Is It Multiplying or Dividing?

▶ Real World Problems

Solve.

Show your work.

26. For a snack, the members of an after school club ate five-eighths of 24 bagels. How many bagels did the group eat?

_____

27. One bag of seed is used to plant $\frac{1}{4}$ acre of corn. How many bags of seed are needed to plant 10 acres of corn?

_____

28. In a staring contest, suppose you stare at your friend for 2 minutes without blinking. Your friend stares at you without blinking for $\frac{9}{10}$ of that time. How long does your friend stare?

_____

29. A car traveled 8 miles in 8 minutes. In that same length of time, a three-toed sloth traveled $\frac{1}{5}$ mile. How many times the sloth's distance did the car travel?

_____

30. Three-fourths of a gallon of milk remains in a jug. Six friends want to share the milk equally. How much milk does each friend receive?

_____

31. A batch of raisin muffins requires $1\frac{1}{4}$ cups of raisins. How many cups of raisins are needed for $2\frac{1}{2}$ batches of muffins?

► Multiplication and Division Practice

Multiply or divide.

32. $\frac{1}{8} \div 2 =$ _____

33. $9 \div 11 =$ _____

34. $2 \cdot 3\frac{1}{2} =$ _____

35. $\frac{2}{3} \cdot \frac{6}{7} =$ _____

36. $\frac{1}{2} \cdot \frac{5}{8} =$ _____

37. $5 \div \frac{1}{5} =$ _____

38. $\frac{1}{12} \div 6 =$ _____

39. $\frac{8}{9} \cdot 3 =$ _____

40. $\frac{2}{3} \cdot 1\frac{1}{2} =$ _____

41. $\frac{1}{7} \div 3 =$ _____

42. $3 \div \frac{1}{7} =$ _____

43. $\frac{4}{5} \cdot \frac{1}{3} =$ _____

44. $\frac{1}{8} \cdot 2 =$ _____

45. $5 \cdot \frac{1}{3} =$ _____

46. $6 \div 5 =$ _____

47. $8 \div \frac{1}{4} =$ _____

48. $\frac{3}{7} \cdot \frac{1}{12} =$ _____

49. $1\frac{1}{3} \cdot 2\frac{1}{3} =$ _____

50. $\frac{1}{10} \div 3 =$ _____

51. $4 \div \frac{1}{3} =$ _____

52. $\frac{6}{7} \cdot \frac{3}{5} =$ _____

▶ Finding an Unknown Factor

1. On Gino's farm, there is a rectangular wooded area in a cornfield. This wooded section has area $\frac{8}{15}$ square mile and is $\frac{2}{3}$ mile long. How wide is the wooded section?

> We can write the division $\frac{8}{15} \div \frac{2}{3} = n$.
>
> This is the same as the unknown-factor multiplication $\frac{2}{3} \cdot n = \frac{8}{15}$.

Step 1
Write an equation.

$$\frac{2}{3} \cdot \frac{?}{?} = \frac{8}{15}$$

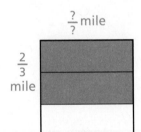

Step 2
Look at the denominators.

$$\frac{2}{3} \cdot \frac{?}{?} = \frac{8}{15}$$
$$3 \cdot 5 = 15$$
$$\frac{?}{?} = \frac{?}{5}$$

Step 3
Look at the numerators.

$$\frac{2}{3} \cdot \frac{?}{5} = \frac{8}{15}$$
$$2 \cdot 4 = 8$$
$$\frac{?}{5} = \frac{4}{5}$$

2. The mugs at a restaurant hold $\frac{2}{3}$ cup of hot chocolate. The restaurant has $\frac{8}{15}$ cup hot chocolate left in its pot. How many servings of $\frac{2}{3}$ cup are in the pot?

Step 1 Write an equation.

$$\frac{?}{?} \cdot \frac{2}{3} = \frac{8}{15}$$

Step 2 Look at the denominators.

Divide each $\frac{1}{3}$ into 5 equal parts to make fifteenths.

$$\frac{?}{5} \cdot \frac{2}{3} = \frac{8}{15}$$

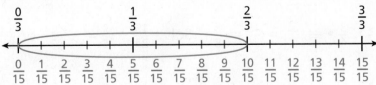

Step 3 Look at the numerators.

Take 4 fifteenths from each of the 2 thirds to make $\frac{8}{15}$.

$$\frac{4}{5} \cdot \frac{2}{3} = \frac{8}{15}$$

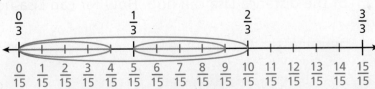

Dividing Numerators and Denominators **125**

Name _____   **Date** _____

Vocabulary

inverse operations

▶ Relating Multiplication and Division

Find the unknown factor in each equation. Then rewrite the multiplication as a division equation.

Multiplication Equation	Related Division Equation
3. $\frac{2}{3} \cdot \dfrac{\square}{\square} = \frac{8}{15}$	$\frac{8}{15} \div \frac{2}{3} = \dfrac{\square}{\square}$
4. $\frac{5}{7} \cdot \dfrac{\square}{\square} = \frac{15}{56}$	$\frac{15}{56} \div \frac{5}{7} = \dfrac{\square}{\square}$
5. $\frac{5}{8} \cdot \dfrac{\square}{\square} = \frac{20}{72}$	
6. $\frac{3}{4} \cdot \dfrac{\square}{\square} = \frac{15}{36}$	

> Multiplication and division are **inverse operations** for all whole numbers, decimals, and fractions. One operation undoes the other.
>
> $$\frac{2}{5} \cdot \frac{1}{5} \div \frac{1}{5} = \frac{2}{5}$$

Divide.

7. $\frac{9}{20} \div \frac{3}{5} =$ _____   8. $\frac{16}{45} \div \frac{2}{9} =$ _____   9. $\frac{6}{45} \div \frac{2}{9} =$ _____

The products in each multiplication equation are simplified. Find the unknown factor. Then choose a related division equation to solve.

10. $\frac{2}{5} \cdot \dfrac{\square}{\square} = \frac{6}{20} = \frac{3}{10}$ Solve $\frac{6}{20} \div \frac{2}{5} = \dfrac{\square}{\square}$ or $\frac{3}{10} \div \frac{2}{5} = \dfrac{\square}{\square}$.

11. $\frac{3}{4} \cdot \dfrac{\square}{\square} = \frac{15}{24} = \frac{5}{8}$ Solve $\frac{15}{24} \div \frac{3}{4} = \dfrac{\square}{\square}$ or $\frac{5}{8} \div \frac{3}{4} = \dfrac{\square}{\square}$.

12. Shaun can hop for $\frac{8}{15}$ of a block. Shaun can hop $\frac{2}{3}$ of the distance Lisa can hop. How far can Lisa hop?

_____

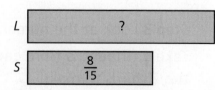

$$S = \frac{2}{3} \cdot L \qquad L = S \div \frac{2}{3}$$

Dividing Numerators and Denominators

► Unsimplify to Divide

$\frac{2}{3} \div \frac{5}{7} = ?$

We cannot divide the numerator of $\frac{2}{3}$ by 5 or the denominator by 7.

To be able to divide, we need to unsimplify $\frac{2}{3}$. To **unsimplify** we rewrite it as an equivalent fraction so the numerators and denominators divide evenly.

$\frac{2}{3} \cdot 1 \cdot 1$

Step 1 $\frac{2}{3} \div \frac{5}{7} = (\frac{2}{3} \cdot \frac{5}{5} \cdot \frac{7}{7}) \div \frac{5}{7}$

$\frac{2}{3}$ unsimplified

1. How is the number you divide $\frac{2}{3}$ by in the original division problem related to the number you multiply $\frac{2}{3}$ by in the final multiplication problem?

_____

_____

$5 \div 5 = 1$

Step 2 $= \frac{2 \cdot 5 \cdot 7}{3 \cdot 5 \cdot 7} \div \frac{5}{7}$

$7 \div 7 = 1$

Step 3 $= \frac{2 \cdot 7}{3 \cdot 5}$

Step 4 $= \frac{2}{3} \cdot \frac{7}{5}$

---

2. Complete.

$\frac{3}{8} \cdot 1 \cdot 1$

Step 1 $\frac{3}{8} \div \frac{2}{5} = (\frac{3}{8} \cdot \frac{2}{2} \cdot \frac{5}{5}) \div \frac{2}{5}$

$\frac{3}{8}$ unsimplified

$2 \div 2 = \underline{\quad}$

Step 2 $= \frac{3 \cdot 2 \cdot 5}{8 \cdot 2 \cdot 5} \div \frac{2}{5}$

$5 \div 5 = \underline{\quad}$

Step 3 $= \frac{3 \cdot 5}{8 \cdot 2}$

Step 4 $= \frac{3}{8} \cdot \frac{\boxed{}}{\boxed{}}$

3. Complete.

$\frac{4}{9} \cdot 1 \cdot 1$

Step 1 $\frac{4}{9} \div \frac{3}{8} = (\frac{4}{9} \cdot \frac{3}{3} \cdot \frac{8}{8}) \div \frac{3}{8}$

$\frac{4}{9}$ unsimplified

$3 \div 3 = \underline{\quad}$

Step 2 $= \frac{4 \cdot 3 \cdot 8}{9 \cdot 3 \cdot 8} \div \frac{3}{8}$

$8 \div 8 = \underline{\quad}$

Step 3 $= \frac{4 \cdot 8}{9 \cdot 3}$

Step 4 $= \frac{4}{9} \cdot \frac{\boxed{}}{\boxed{}}$

Summary: When dividing fractions, unsimplifying the dividend and then dividing numerators and denominators is the same as multiplying by the reciprocal of the divisor. For example, $\frac{2}{3} \div \frac{5}{7} = \frac{2}{3} \cdot \frac{7}{5}$.

▶ Divide by Either Method

**Divide either by dividing numerators and denominators
or by multiplying by the reciprocal of the divisor.**

4. $\frac{1}{10} \div \frac{2}{3}$ _____

5. $\frac{15}{12} \div \frac{5}{6}$ _____

6. $\frac{2}{3} \div \frac{3}{4}$ _____

7. $2\frac{1}{4} \div \frac{3}{4}$ _____

8. $\frac{15}{16} \div \frac{5}{4}$ _____

9. $2\frac{1}{5} \div \frac{2}{3}$ _____

10. $\frac{2}{7} \div \frac{3}{4}$ _____

11. $\frac{4}{10} \div \frac{4}{5}$ _____

12. $\frac{5}{6} \div \frac{4}{5}$ _____

13. $1\frac{3}{8} \div \frac{1}{2}$ _____

14. $\frac{18}{24} \div \frac{9}{12}$ _____

15. $2\frac{1}{4} \div 1\frac{1}{2}$ _____

16. Choose a problem from Exercises 4–15 that you solved
    by dividing numerators and dividing denominators.
    Solve it again, but this time multiply by the reciprocal
    of the divisor. Do you get the same answer?

_____

The following division methods give the same answer:

Method 1: Dividing numerators and dividing denominators.

Method 2: Multiplying by the reciprocal of the divisor.

Dividing by Unsimplifying

▶ Divide by Multiplying by the Reciprocal

You can solve any division problem involving two fractions or a fraction and a whole number by multiplying by the reciprocal of the divisor.

You know that you can think of a division problem like this:

product ÷ known factor = unknown factor

To divide you multiply by the reciprocal of the known factor.

Think: "Flip the factor and multiply."

Study the examples and discuss them with your class.

Example 1	**Example 2**
fraction ÷ fraction	whole number ÷ unit fraction
$\frac{5}{6} \div \frac{2}{3} = \frac{5}{\cancel{6}_2} \cdot \frac{\cancel{3}^1}{2} = \frac{5}{4}$ or $1\frac{1}{4}$	$8 \div \frac{1}{4} = \frac{8}{1} \div \frac{1}{4} = \frac{8}{1} \cdot \frac{4}{1} = 32$

Example 3	**Example 4**
unit fraction ÷ whole number	whole number ÷ fraction
$\frac{1}{4} \div 8 = \frac{1}{4} \div \frac{8}{1} = \frac{1}{4} \cdot \frac{1}{8} = \frac{1}{32}$	$5 \div \frac{3}{4} = \frac{5}{1} \div \frac{3}{4} = \frac{5}{1} \cdot \frac{4}{3} = \frac{20}{3}$ or $6\frac{2}{3}$

Example 5	**Example 6**
fraction ÷ whole number	fraction ÷ unit fraction
$\frac{3}{4} \div 5 = \frac{3}{4} \div \frac{5}{1} = \frac{3}{4} \cdot \frac{1}{5} = \frac{3}{20}$	$\frac{2}{3} \div \frac{1}{12} = \frac{2}{\cancel{3}_1} \cdot \frac{\cancel{12}^4}{1} = 8$

Example 7
unit fraction ÷ fraction
$\frac{1}{12} \div \frac{2}{3} = \frac{1}{\cancel{12}_4} \cdot \frac{\cancel{3}^1}{2} = \frac{1}{8}$

▶ Practice Dividing Fractions

Divide using any method.

1. $\frac{3}{4} \div \frac{5}{2}$ _____

2. $\frac{3}{4} \div 5$ _____

3. $\frac{8}{25} \div \frac{4}{5}$ _____

4. $\frac{3}{4} \div \frac{1}{5}$ _____

5. $\frac{7}{8} \div \frac{5}{8}$ _____

6. $\frac{1}{21} \div \frac{1}{7}$ _____

7. $3 \div \frac{1}{7}$ _____

8. $3 \div \frac{4}{7}$ _____

Solve.

Show your work.

9. Marilla's dress had $1\frac{5}{6}$ yards of blue lace around it. Her sister Ana's dress had $\frac{3}{4}$ yard of purple lace around it. Marilla's lace is how many times as long as Ana's lace?

_____

10. Ms. Padilla divided $\frac{3}{4}$ liter of apricot juice into 5 glasses for her family. How much did each person get?

_____

11. The sixth grade garden at Sunnyside School is $\frac{4}{3}$ yards long and has an area of $\frac{8}{9}$ square yard. How wide is the garden?

_____

12. Bronwyn's prize-winning yellow zucchini is $1\frac{1}{6}$ feet long. This is $\frac{3}{4}$ the length of her prize-winning green zucchini. How long is the green zucchini?

_____

13. A pot contains $5\frac{1}{3}$ cups of oatmeal. How many $\frac{3}{4}$-cup servings is this? How much will be left over?

_____

Dividing by Multiplying by the Reciprocal

▶ Predict, Solve, and Check

Will each product or quotient below be greater or less than the first fraction? Circle your prediction, and then find the actual product or quotient to check your prediction.

1. $\frac{3}{4} \cdot \frac{6}{5}$ Predict: $> \frac{3}{4}$ or $< \frac{3}{4}$

   $\frac{3}{4} \cdot \frac{6}{5} =$ _____

2. $\frac{2}{3} \cdot \frac{3}{5}$ Predict: $> \frac{2}{3}$ or $< \frac{2}{3}$

   $\frac{2}{3} \cdot \frac{3}{5} =$ _____

3. $\frac{9}{10} \div \frac{6}{5}$ Predict: $> \frac{9}{10}$ or $< \frac{9}{10}$

   $\frac{9}{10} \div \frac{6}{5} =$ _____

4. $\frac{3}{10} \div \frac{2}{5}$ Predict: $> \frac{3}{10}$ or $< \frac{3}{10}$

   $\frac{3}{10} \div \frac{2}{5} =$ _____

Solve.

5. Four friends discovered $\frac{3}{4}$ of a pizza in the refrigerator and ate $\frac{2}{3}$ of it for a snack. What fraction did they eat?

   a. What fraction is $\frac{3}{4}$ being multiplied by? _____

   b. Is the fraction in Part a greater or less than 1? _____

   c. Will the product be greater or less than $\frac{3}{4}$? _____

   d. What fraction of the pizza did the friends eat? _____

6. A baker placed $4\frac{2}{3}$ cups of bread flour into small plastic containers that each had a capacity of $\frac{2}{3}$ cup. How many containers did the baker fill?

   a. What fraction is $4\frac{2}{3}$ being divided by? _____

   b. Is the fraction in Part a greater or less than 1? _____

   c. Will the quotient be greater or less than $4\frac{2}{3}$? _____

   d. How many containers did the baker fill? _____

Name _____ Date _____

▶ Real World Problems

Decide if you need to multiply or divide. Then solve. *Show your work.*

7. Todd used $\frac{2}{3}$ cup of oatmeal for a muffin recipe. To make a different recipe, he needs only $\frac{3}{4}$ of that amount. What amount of oatmeal does the different recipe require?

_____

8. Amelia is using a wheelbarrow to move $1\frac{1}{2}$ cubic yards of topsoil. The capacity of the wheelbarrow is $\frac{1}{6}$ cubic yard. How many wheelbarrow loads will be needed to move the soil?

_____

9. A rectangular field measures $\frac{3}{10}$ mile by $\frac{1}{6}$ mile. In square miles, what is the area of the field?

_____

10. A pitcher contains $\frac{7}{16}$ gallon of lemonade. How many cups, each having a $\frac{1}{12}$-gallon capacity, can be filled from the jug?

_____

11. Carlos jogs the same route each day. The route is $3\frac{1}{4}$ miles long, and he stops to rest every $\frac{7}{8}$ mile. How many times does Carlos stop to rest during his jog?

_____

12. Last night Julian needed $\frac{5}{12}$ hour to complete his homework. Aaliyah needed only $\frac{4}{5}$ as long. How many *minutes* did it take Aaliyah to complete her homework?

Is It Multiplying or Dividing?

▶ Fraction Mixed Review

Solve.

Show your work.

13. The table at the right uses fractions and mixed numbers to represent the weights and costs of peaches that can be purchased at a roadside fruit stand.

   Complete the table.

Weight (pounds)	Cost (dollars)
$\frac{3}{4}$	
1	$3\frac{3}{5}$
	$4\frac{1}{2}$
$1\frac{5}{8}$	

14. A triangle has a base measure of $5\frac{1}{2}$ centimeters and a height of $2\frac{1}{2}$ centimeters. What is the area of the triangle? Use a mixed number in simplest form in your answer.

_____

15. Quinn knows that the area of a triangle is $\frac{1}{18}$ square yard and its base measures $\frac{1}{9}$ yard. What is the height of the triangle?

_____

Simplify before multiplying.

16. $\frac{14}{8} \cdot \frac{32}{42} = $ _____

17. $\frac{44}{36} \cdot \frac{72}{33} = $ _____

18. $\frac{16}{24} \cdot \frac{15}{28} = $ _____

19. $\frac{14}{25} \cdot \frac{27}{32} \cdot \frac{35}{21} \cdot \frac{64}{8} = $ _____

20. $\frac{32}{18} \cdot \frac{21}{20} \cdot \frac{15}{32} \cdot \frac{8}{49} = $ _____

▶ What's the Error?

Dear Math Students,

To find the product at the right, I followed the steps below. $\boxed{2\frac{1}{3} \cdot 1\frac{3}{7}}$

Step 1: Multiply the whole numbers. $2 \cdot 1 = 2$

Step 2: Multiply the fractions. $\frac{1}{\cancel{3}} \cdot \frac{\cancel{3}^1}{7} = \frac{1}{7}$

Step 3: Add the results from Step 1 and Step 2. $2 + \frac{1}{7} = 2\frac{1}{7}$

I learned that $2\frac{1}{7}$ was not the correct product. Please explain my mistake, and how I can find the correct product.

Your friend,
Puzzled Penguin

21. _____

_____

_____

Dear Math Students,

To find the quotient at the right, I followed the steps below. $\boxed{3\frac{3}{4} \div 1\frac{1}{3}}$

Step 1: Change the mixed numbers to fractions. $3\frac{3}{4} = \frac{15}{4}$ and $1\frac{1}{3} = \frac{4}{3}$

Step 2: Multiply the fractions. $\frac{\cancel{15}^5}{\cancel{4}_1} \cdot \frac{\cancel{4}^1}{\cancel{3}_1} = \frac{5}{1} = 5$

I was told that 5 is not the correct quotient. Please explain my mistake, and how I can find the correct quotient.

Your friend,
Puzzled Penguin

22. _____

_____

_____

Is It Multiplying or Dividing?

▶ Review Operations with Fractions and Decimals

To add, subtract, or compare fractions and decimals, use $1 = \frac{D}{D}$ to make equivalent fractions or decimals with the same denominator.

$\frac{2}{3} + \frac{4}{5} = \frac{5}{5} \cdot \frac{2}{3} + \frac{3}{3} \cdot \frac{4}{5} = \frac{10}{15} + \frac{12}{15} = \frac{22}{15}$ $0.2 + 0.04 = 0.20 + 0.04 = 0.24$

$\frac{2}{10} \cdot \frac{10}{10} = \frac{20}{100}$

$\frac{4}{5} - \frac{2}{3} = \frac{3}{3} \cdot \frac{4}{5} - \frac{5}{5} \cdot \frac{2}{3} = \frac{12}{15} - \frac{10}{15} = \frac{2}{15}$ $0.2 - 0.04 = 0.20 - 0.04 = 0.16$

To multiply fractions, multiply the numerators and multiply the denominators.

$\frac{2}{3} \cdot \frac{4}{5} = \frac{8}{15}$

To multiply decimals, multiply the numbers and count decimal places in the factors to place the decimal point in the product.

$0.2 \cdot 0.4 = 0.08$

$\frac{2}{10} \cdot \frac{4}{10} = \frac{8}{100}$

To divide fractions, divide the numerators and divide the denominators or multiply by the reciprocal.

$\frac{8}{15} \div \frac{2}{3} = \frac{8 \div 2}{15 \div 3} = \frac{4}{5}$ $\frac{8}{15} \div \frac{2}{3} = \frac{8}{15} \cdot \frac{3}{2} = \frac{24}{30}$ or $\frac{4}{5}$

To divide decimals, unsimplify using $1 = \frac{D}{D}$ to make the divisor a whole number, or move the decimal points the same number of places.

$0.08 \div 0.2 = \frac{0.08}{0.2} \cdot \frac{10}{10} = \frac{0.8}{2} = 0.4$ $0.2\overline{)0.08}$ $\overset{0.4}{}$

Simplify.

1. $\frac{3}{4} + \frac{5}{8}$ _____

2. $\frac{5}{6} \cdot \frac{2}{3}$ _____

3. $3\frac{7}{8} - \frac{1}{2}$ _____

4. $7.6 - 1.81$ _____

5. $2.29 + 0.8$ _____

6. $5.2 \cdot 1.5$ _____

7. $1\frac{2}{5} + \frac{7}{8}$ _____

8. $0.27 \div 0.6$ _____

9. $\frac{1}{3} + 6\frac{7}{10}$ _____

▶ Choose the Operation

Write and solve an equation.

Show your work.

10. Hala can ride her bike $7\frac{1}{2}$ miles in an hour. How far will she ride in 3 hours? How far will she ride in $\frac{2}{3}$ of an hour?

11. Jonny can throw a baseball $30\frac{1}{3}$ yards. Joey can throw a baseball $33\frac{1}{2}$ yards. How much farther can Joey throw?

12. Eryn's rabbit eats $\frac{5}{16}$ pound of food each day. Eryn buys food in 5-pound bags. How many days of food are in a bag?

13. Marcus has soccer practice for 9 hours each week. Luis spends $\frac{5}{6}$ as much time practicing soccer. How much time each week does Luis spend practicing?

14. In a long jump competition, Stacey jumped 10 feet, which was 0.75 foot farther than Reggie jumped. How far did Reggie jump?

15. Evan bought $\frac{3}{8}$ pound of sunflower seeds and $\frac{3}{16}$ pound of thistle seeds for his bird feeder. How many pounds of seeds did he buy?

16. Casandra's fish bowl holds 0.9 gallon. The bowl is $\frac{3}{4}$ full. How much water is in the bowl?

17. Ty practices trumpet for $1\frac{2}{3}$ hours every day. He plays scales every $\frac{1}{3}$ hour. How often during a practice does Ty play scales?

▶ Math and the Stock Market

Many people save for retirement by making investments. One example of an investment is to buy shares of stock in a company. Companies use the money they receive from the sale of stock for operating expenses. Most companies have operating expenses of millions or billions of dollars.

When you buy shares of stock in a company, you become a shareholder, which is a part-owner of the company. Shares of stock are bought and sold on a stock exchange like the one shown at the right.

The following terms and definitions are related to buying and selling shares of stock.

Dividend A portion of a company's profits that are paid to shareholders. Dividends are often paid quarterly.

Sales The number of shares sold that day.

High The highest price per share that day.

Low The lowest price per share that day.

Last The price per share for the last sale of the day.

Change The increase or decrease from the price at the end of the previous day.

Stock prices can be given as fractions or decimals.

Name	Dividend	Sales	High	Low	Last	Change
Alphabet Foods	–	72,500	$6.44	$6.39	$6.44	$^+$$0.02
Colossal Corp.	$0.30	440,000	$14\frac{5}{8}$	$14\frac{1}{4}$	$14\frac{1}{2}$	$^-\frac{1}{8}$

▶ Buying Stocks

The table below shows the cost of one share of the stock
of two different companies.

Company Name	Monday Price	Tuesday Price	Wednesday Price	Thursday Price	Friday Price
Exploration Inc.	$8\frac{1}{4}$	$8\frac{1}{8}$	$8\frac{5}{8}$	$8\frac{1}{2}$	$8\frac{3}{4}$
Miles of Styles	$12.04	$12.03	$12.05	$12.02	$11.98

1. Suppose you purchase 125 shares of each company's stock
   on Monday. Write an equation that represents the cost (c)
   of each purchase in dollars. Then solve each equation.

   _____

   _____

2. Find the change in price for a share of each company's
   stock during the times shown below. Write + to indicate
   an increase in price and write − to indicate a decrease.

   a. from Monday to Tuesday _____

   b. from Tuesday to Wednesday _____

   c. from Wednesday to Thursday _____

   d. from Thursday to Friday _____

3. Suppose you sell your 125 shares on Friday. Calculate the
   amount of money you should receive for each stock. Did
   you earn a profit, or lose money?

   _____

   _____

4. Suppose you had purchased 12,500 shares of each company's
   stock instead of 125. How would your profit or loss for
   each stock change? Use a calculator to help decide.

   _____

Focus on Mathematical Practices

▶ Vocabulary

Choose the best term from the box.

1. In the division exercise 56 ÷ 8, the number 56 is the

   _____. (Lesson 3-1)

2. $\frac{6}{18}$ and $\frac{3}{9}$ are _____. (Lesson 3-7)

3. 24 is the _____ of 12 and 8.
   (Lesson 3-9)

▶ Concepts and Skills

Complete.

4. Why is this problem a division problem?

   The rectangular floor of a playpen has an area of 14 square feet
   and the rectangle has a base of $3\frac{1}{2}$ feet. What is the height of
   the rectangle? (Lesson 3-5)

   _____

   _____

   _____

5. Without doing any computation, explain why 73 ÷ 0.42 is
   greater than 0.42 • 73. (Lesson 3-5)

   _____

   _____

   _____

Multiply or divide. (Lessons 3-1, 3-2, 3-3, 3-4, 3-5)

6. $2\overline{)629}$ 7. $25\overline{)2,515}$ 8. $7.5\overline{)0.9}$ 9. $0.35\overline{)7}$

10. $\begin{array}{r} 0.4 \\ \times\ 0.3 \\ \hline \end{array}$ 11. $\begin{array}{r} 0.06 \\ \times\ 12 \\ \hline \end{array}$ 12. $\begin{array}{r} 5.8 \\ \times\ 2.5 \\ \hline \end{array}$ 13. $\begin{array}{r} 2.9 \\ \times\ 0.81 \\ \hline \end{array}$

Rewrite the fractions as equivalent fractions with a common denominator. Use the LCM of the denominators. (Lesson 3-9)

14. $\frac{2}{7}$, $\frac{1}{3}$ _____

15. $\frac{5}{12}$, $\frac{3}{4}$ _____

16. $\frac{7}{10}$, $\frac{4}{15}$ _____

Add or subtract. (Lessons 3-6, 3-7, 3-8, 3-9)

17. $\frac{7}{9} + \frac{5}{6}$ _____

18. $3\frac{2}{5} - 1\frac{9}{10}$ _____

19. $2.6 - 1.78$ _____

Multiply or divide. (Lessons 3-10, 3-11, 3-12, 3-13, 3-14, 3-15, 3-16, 3-17)

20. $\frac{8}{15} \div \frac{4}{5}$ _____

21. $\frac{3}{4} \div 7$ _____

22. $1\frac{1}{2} \cdot 1\frac{3}{8}$ _____

▶ Problem Solving

Solve. (Lessons 3-3, 3-5, 3-13, 3-14, 3-15, 3-16, 3-17)

23. Darnell is sewing a strip of cloth made from a red section and a blue section. He needs a red section that is 3.75 cm long and a blue section that is $\frac{1}{5}$ the length of the red section. What is the total length of the whole strip?

_____

24. How many $\frac{3}{4}$-cup servings are in $8\frac{1}{2}$ cups of juice?

_____

25. **Extended Response** Dana's dog Skippy weighs 20.4 pounds. Her cat Bruiser weighs 0.75 as much as Skippy.

Does Bruiser weigh more or less than Skippy? Explain how you know.

_____

_____

_____

How much does Bruiser weigh?

_____

Family Letter

Dear Family,

In this unit, students are studying the surface area of prisms and pyramids. **Surface area** is the sum of the areas of all the faces of a geometric figure. Your student will make nets to visualize the parts that make up the surface area of a prism or pyramid and learn a systematic approach to finding the total surface area of the solid figure.

Rectangular Prism Net   Rectangular Prism

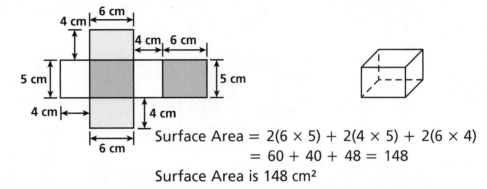

Surface Area = $2(6 \times 5) + 2(4 \times 5) + 2(6 \times 4)$
$= 60 + 40 + 48 = 148$
Surface Area is 148 cm²

The types of prisms and pyramids that students will be calculating the surface areas for are shown below.

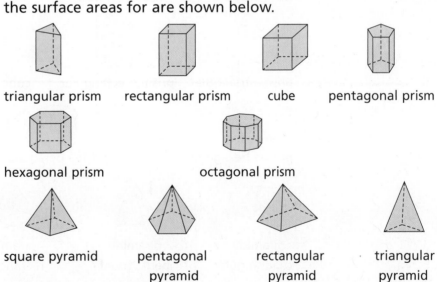

triangular prism   rectangular prism   cube   pentagonal prism

hexagonal prism   octagonal prism

square pyramid   pentagonal pyramid   rectangular pyramid   triangular pyramid

Students will also explore real-life applications of surface area.

If you need practice materials or if you have any questions, please call or write to me.

Sincerely,
Your child's teacher

COMMON CORE This unit includes the Common Core Standards for Mathematical Content for Geometry and Algebra, CC.6.G.1, CC.6.G.4, CC.6.EE.2, CC.6.EE.2c and all Mathematical Practices.

Carta a la familia

Estimada familia,

En esta unidad, los estudiantes aprenderán a calcular el área total de los prismas y las pirámides. El **área total** es la suma de las áreas de las caras de una figura geométrica. Los estudiantes harán plantillas para visualizar las partes que forman el área total de un prisma o una pirámide y aprenderán un método para hallar la superficie total del cuerpo geométrico.

Plantilla de prisma rectangular   Prisma rectangular

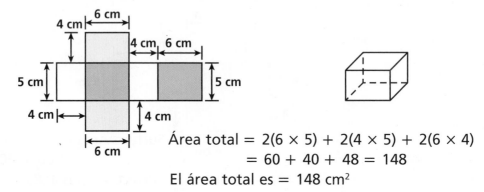

Área total = $2(6 \times 5) + 2(4 \times 5) + 2(6 \times 4)$
= $60 + 40 + 48 = 148$
El área total es = 148 cm²

Los estudiantes calcularán el área total de los tipos de prismas y pirámides que se muestran abajo.

prisma triangular   prisma rectangular   cubo   prisma pentagonal

prisma hexagonal   prisma octagonal

pirámide   pirámide   pirámide   pirámide
cuadrangular   pentagonal   rectangular   triangular

Los estudiantes también explorarán situaciones de la vida real en las que se aplica lo que han aprendido acerca del área total.

Si necesita materiales para practicar o si tiene preguntas, por favor comuníquese conmigo.

Sinceramente,
El maestro de su hijo

COMMON CORE

Esta unidad incluye los Common Core Standards for Mathematical Content for Geometry and Algebra, CC.6.G.1, CC.6.G.4, CC.6.EE.2, CC.6.EE.2c and all Mathematical Practices.

Name _____   Date _____

► Rectangular Prism Net

A **net** is a two-dimensional flat pattern that can be folded into a three-dimensional figure.

Cut out the net and form the solid figure.

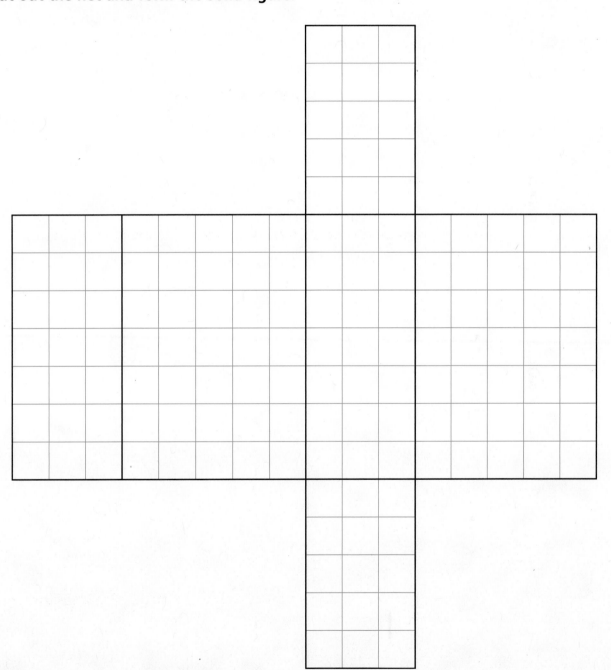

Nets and Surface Area for Rectangular Prisms

Vocabulary

prism
face
rectangular prism
base
lateral face
edge
vertex

▶ Make a Rectangular Prism from a Net

1. The flat rectangular sides of a **prism** are called **faces**.
   How many faces does a **rectangular prism** have?

   _____

2. Two parallel faces of a prism are called **bases**.
   What shape are the bases of a rectangular prism?

   _____

3. The faces that are not bases are called **lateral faces**.
   What shape are the lateral faces?

   _____

Place your rectangular prism in the same position as
shown in the picture below on the right.

Use your rectangular prism to answer questions 4–6.

4. What are the dimensions of the bases of your
   rectangular prism?

   _____

5. What are the dimensions of the lateral faces?

   _____

   _____

6. Record the dimensions of the prism you made on
   the picture at the right.

   _____

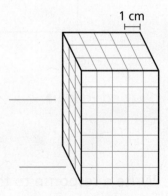

1 cm

▶ What's the Error?

Dear Math Students,

Today I made this net for a rectangular prism. Before I trace this net on cardboard, can you tell me if the net will form a rectangular prism? If not, can you tell me what I did wrong?

Your friend,

Puzzled Penguin

7. Write a response to the Puzzled Penguin.

_____

_____

_____

Name   Date

▶ Draw a Net for a Rectangular Prism

**Draw a net for a rectangular prism. Then cut out the net
and form a rectangular prism.**

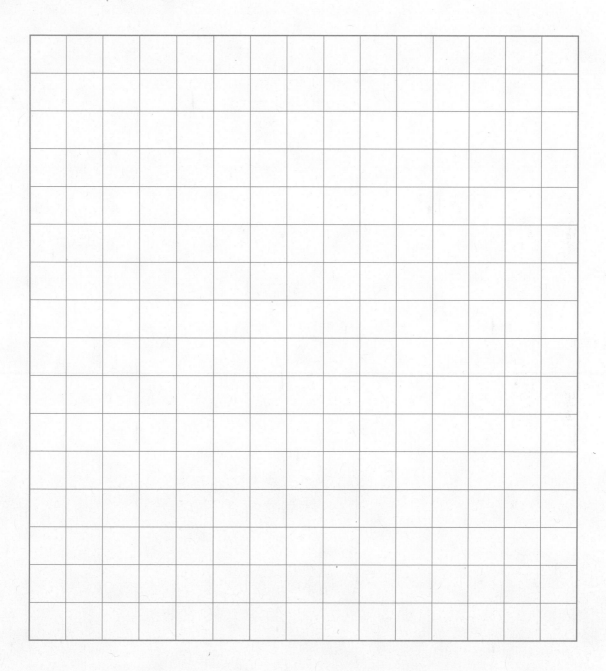

▶ Draw a Net for a Rectangular Prism (continued)

Vocabulary

surface area

▶ Find Surface Area Using Nets

The net on the left forms the rectangular prism on the right. Fill in the missing dimensions. Then find the surface area of each rectangular prism.

8.

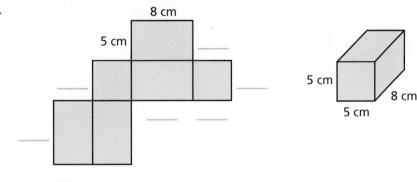

Area of a square base: _____   Area of a rectangular face: _____

Surface area: _____

9.

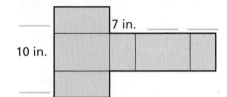

Area of top rectangular face: _____

Area of side rectangular face: _____

Area of front rectangular face: _____

Surface area: _____

10. How can you find the surface area of any rectangular prism?

_____

_____

11. Use the rectangular prism at the right to write an expression to show how you can find the surface area of any rectangular prism.

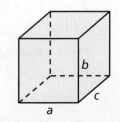

_____

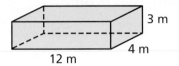

▶ Find Surface Area

Find the surface area.

12.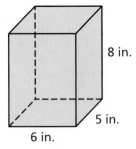
3 m
12 m
4 m

13.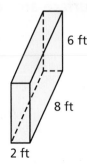
6 ft
8 ft
2 ft

14.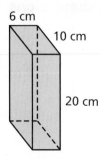
6 cm
10 cm
20 cm

_____

_____

_____

15.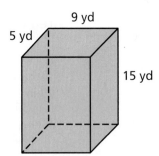
8 in.
5 in.
6 in.

16.
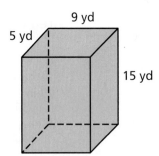
9 yd
5 yd
15 yd

17.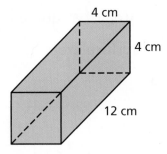
4 cm
4 cm
12 cm

_____

_____

_____

Solve.

Show your work

18. Jenna wants to paint a wooden jewelry box that is 8 inches by 6 inches by 3 inches with clear paint. The bottle of paint says it will cover a total area of 250 square inches. Does she have enough to cover the entire box? Explain.

_____

19. Rico is making a rectangular paper lantern that is 28 cm by 15 cm by 12 cm. He plans to cover the faces of the lantern with paper that comes in sheets that have an area of 9 cm^2 and cost $0.08 a sheet. How much will it cost to cover the six faces of the lantern?

_____

Vocabulary

cube

▶ Identify Cube Nets

A **cube** is a rectangular prism that has six congruent square faces.

Put a check mark next to each net that will form a cube. Fix the other nets so they will form a cube.

20.

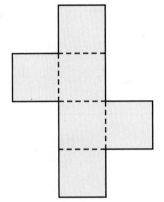

21.

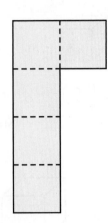

22.

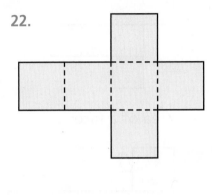

23.

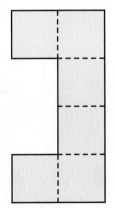

24.

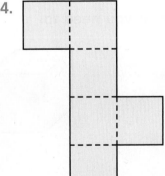

25.

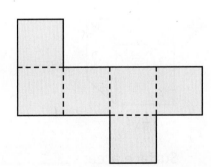

▶ Fractional Edge Lengths

**The net on the left forms the rectangular prism on the right.
Fill in the missing dimensions. Then find the area of a face
and the surface area of each cube.**

26.

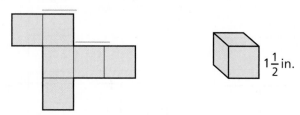

$1\frac{1}{2}$ in.

Area of a face: _____   Surface area: _____

27.

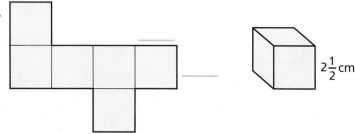

$2\frac{1}{2}$ cm

Area of a face: _____   Surface area: _____

Find the surface area. Draw a net if you need to.

28.

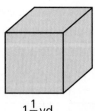

$1\frac{1}{3}$ yd

Surface area: _____

29.

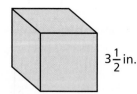

$3\frac{1}{2}$ in.

Surface area: _____

30. How can you find the surface area of any cube?

_____

_____

s

31. Use the cube at the right to write an expression to show how
you can find the surface area of any cube.

_____

Nets and Surface Area for Rectangular Prisms

Name _____   **Date** _____

▶ Make Nonrectangular Prisms

Cut out the polygons from this page and the rectangles from
the next page to make nonrectangular prisms.

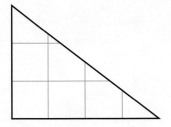

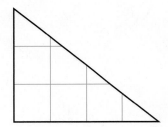

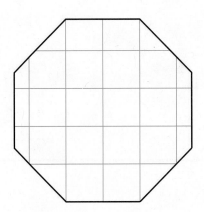

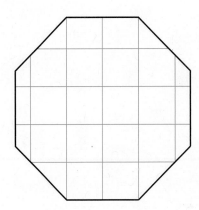

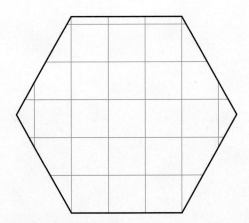

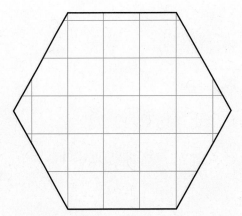

► Make Nonrectangular Prisms (continued)

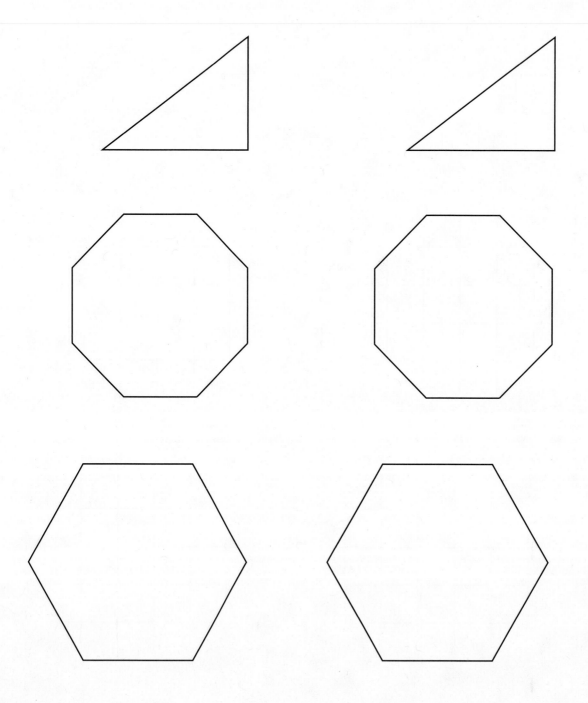

Nets and Surface Area for Nonrectangular Prisms

Name _____ Date _____

► Make Nonrectangular Prisms (continued)

For triangular prism   For octagonal prism   For hexagonal prism

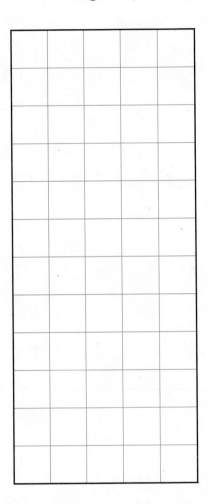

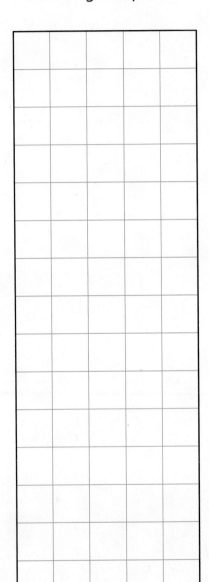

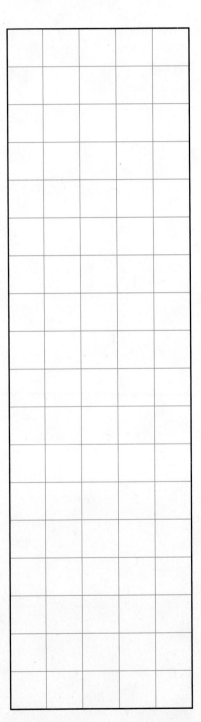

Nets and Surface Area for Nonrectangular Prisms **149C**

▶ Make Nonrectangular Prisms (continued)

Nets and Surface Area for Nonrectangular Prisms

Name   Date

▶ Draw a Net for a Nonrectangular Prism

Draw a net for a nonrectangular prism. Then cut out the net and form a nonrectangular prism.

▶ Identify Prisms

Write the shape of the base and use it to name the prism.

1.

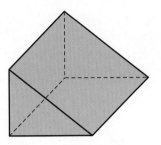

Base: _____

Name: _____

2.

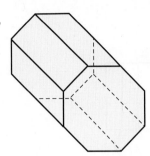

Base: _____

Name: _____

3.

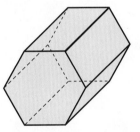

Base: _____

Name: _____

4.

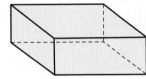

Base: _____

Name: _____

5.

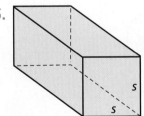

Base: _____

Name: _____

6.

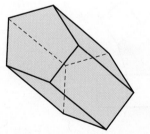

Base: _____

Name: _____

7. What do you notice about the name of the base and the name of the prism?

_____

8. How is a prism named? _____

▶ Match Nets and Solids

Match each net in the first column to a solid in the second column.

9. _____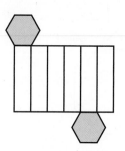
             A.

10. _____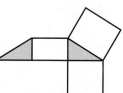
             B.

11. _____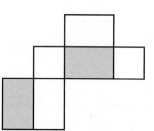
             C.

12. _____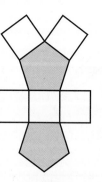
             D.

13. _____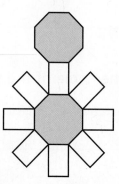
             E.

▶ **What's the Error?**

Dear Math Students,

I designed some shipping boxes with no overlapping cardboard. I found that it takes 444 in.^{2} to make this box. Is my answer correct? If not, can you tell me what I did wrong?

Your friend,

Puzzled Penguin

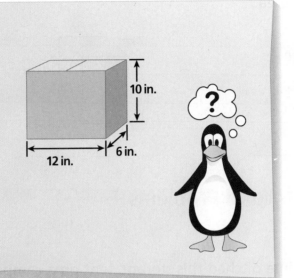

1. Write a response to the Puzzled Penguin.

_____

_____

_____

Dear Math Students,

Here is another shipping box I invented with no overlapping cardboard. I found that it takes 228 in.^{2} to make this box. Is my answer correct? If not, can you tell me what I did wrong?

Your friend,

Puzzled Penguin

2. Write a response to the Puzzled Penguin.

_____

_____

_____

▶ Find the Surface Area

Find the surface area.

3.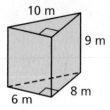
10 m
9 m
8 m
6 m

_____

4.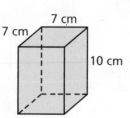
7 cm
7 cm
10 cm

_____

5.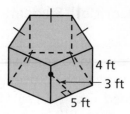
4 ft
3 ft
5 ft

_____

▶ Solve Real World Problems

Solve.

6. Harry and Jaime pitched this storage tent on a camping trip. How many square feet of canvas did it take to make the tent?

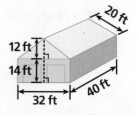
13 ft
12 ft
16 ft
10 ft

_____

7. Rita bought this storage cube for her room. How many square inches of wood did it take to make the storage cube?

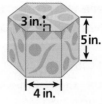
16 in.
16 in.
16 in.

_____

8. Erin made this jewelry box with a regular hexagon for the top and bottom. How many square inches of cardboard did she use?

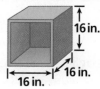
3 in.
5 in.
4 in.

_____

9. Kent bought a hat that came in this box. How many square inches of cardboard did it take to make this hatbox and top?

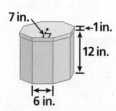
7 in.
1 in.
12 in.
6 in.

_____

10. A contractor needs to know how many square feet of metal it takes to build this warehouse including the roof. The warehouse will have a concrete floor. How many square feet of metal does he need?

20 ft
12 ft
14 ft
32 ft
40 ft

_____

Surface Area of Prisms

4–4
Class Activity

Name _____

Date _____

▶ Make a Pyramid

Cut out the net and form the solid figure.

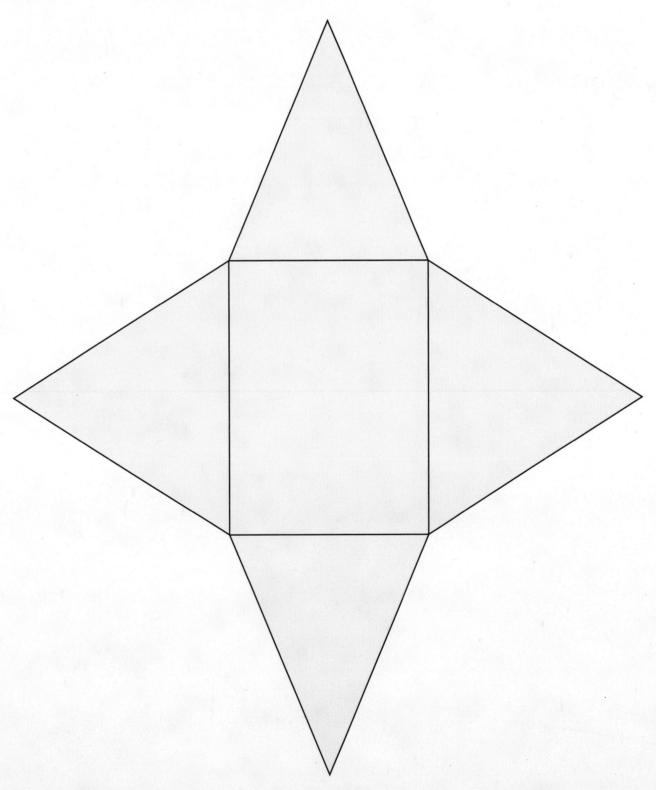

▶ Make a Pyramid (continued)

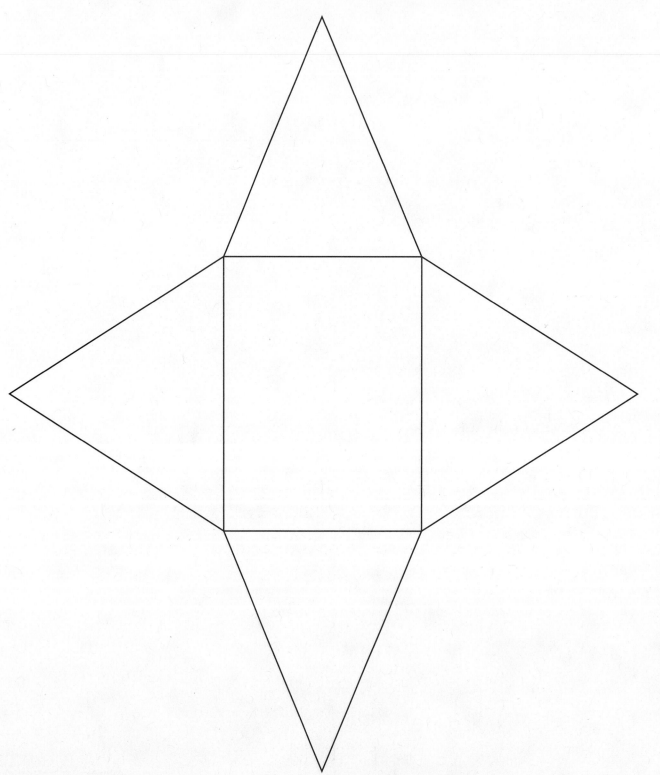

Nets for Pyramids

▶ Make Another Pyramid

Cut out the net and form the solid figure.

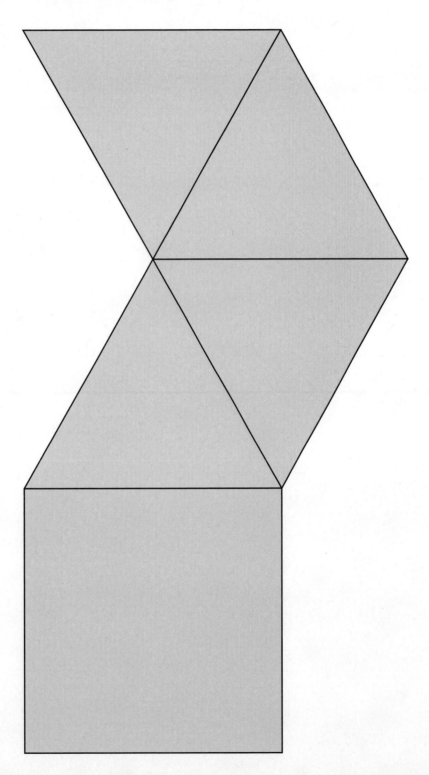

► Make Another Pyramid (continued)

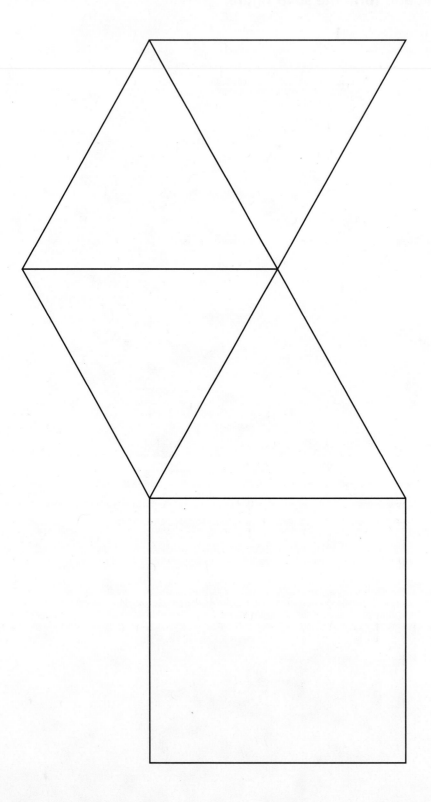

Nets for Pyramids

▶ Draw a Net for a Pyramid

Draw a net for a pyramid. Then cut out the net and form the pyramid.

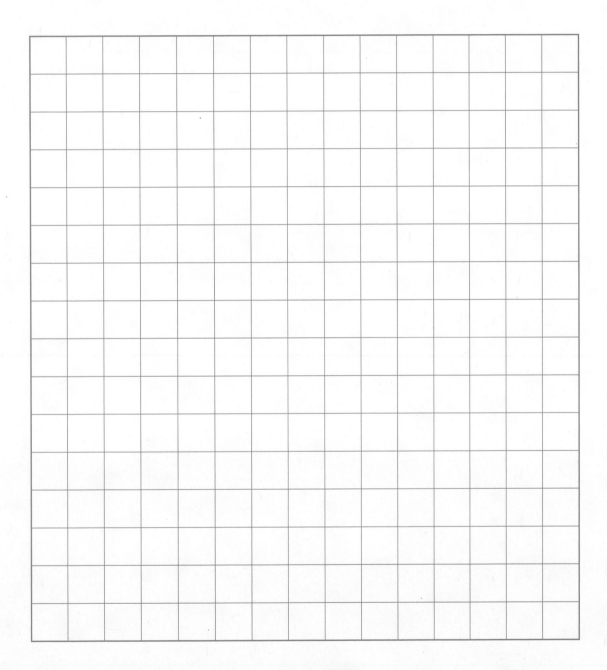

▶ Draw a Net for a Pyramid (continued)

▶ Make Pyramids with Other Bases

Cut out the polygons from this page and the triangles from the next page to form pyramids.

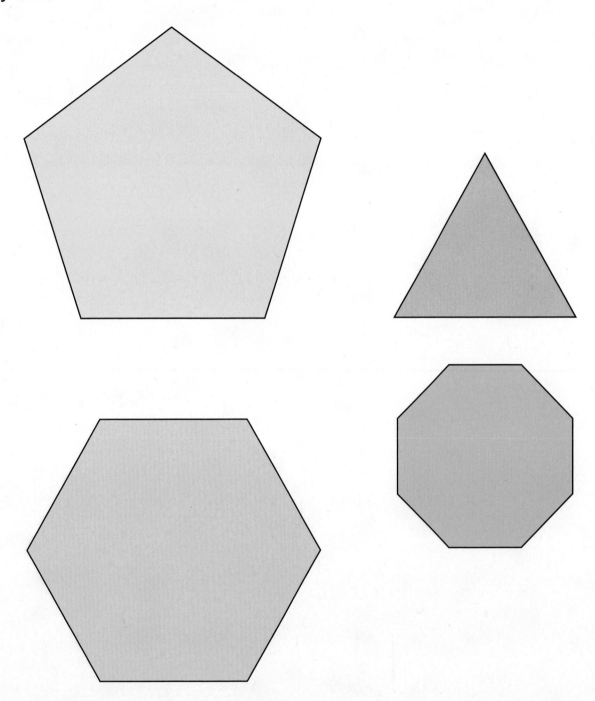

▶ Make Pyramids with Other Bases (continued)

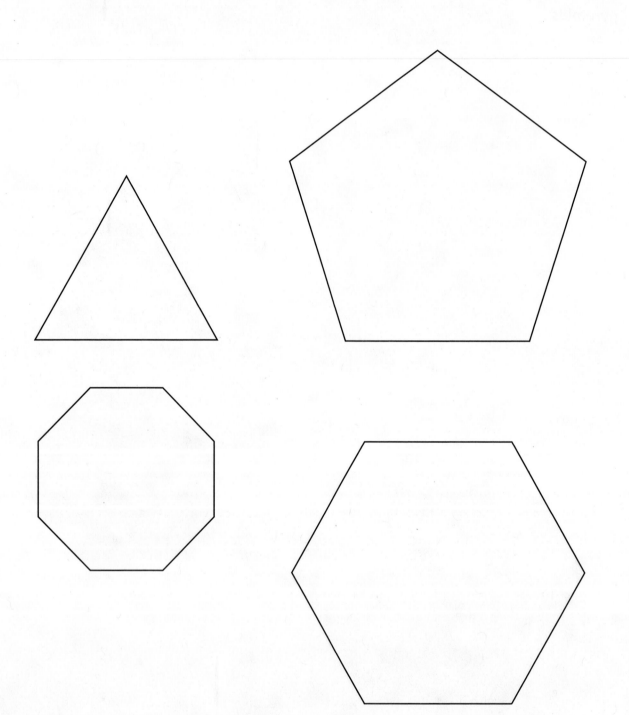

Nets for Pyramids

Name _____ **Date** _____

Vocabulary
slant height

▶ Make Pyramids with Other Bases (continued)

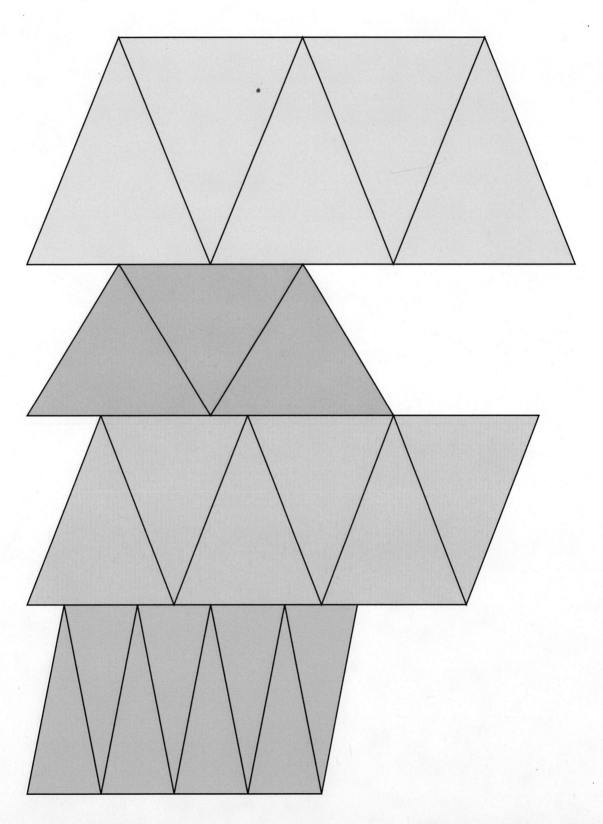

► Make Pyramids with Other Bases (continued)

Vocabulary

pyramid
base
face

▶ Discuss Pyramids

A **pyramid** is a solid whose **base** can be any polygon and whose other **faces** are triangles that meet at a point.

Name the shape of the base and use it to name the pyramid.

1.

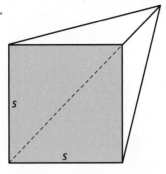

Base: _____

Name: _____

2.

Base: _____

Name: _____

3.

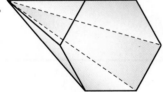

Base: _____

Name: _____

4.

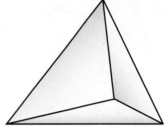

Base: _____

Name: _____

5.

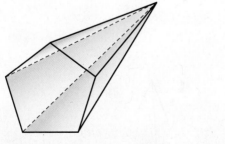

Base: _____

Name: _____

6.

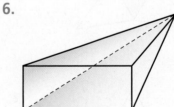

Base: _____

Name: _____

▶ Pyramids and Nets

Match each net to a solid.

7. _____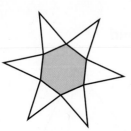

8. _____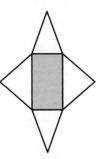

9. _____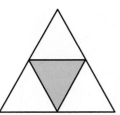

10. _____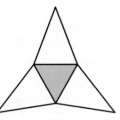

11. _____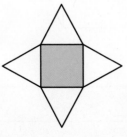

A.

B.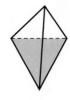

C.

D.

E.

▶ Find Surface Area

These nets form pyramids. Find the surface area of each net.

1.

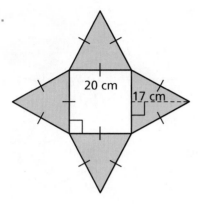

20 cm
17 cm

_____

2.

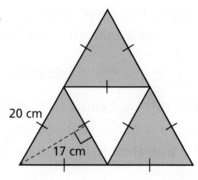

20 cm
17 cm

_____

3.

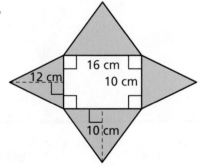

16 cm
12 cm
10 cm
10 cm

_____

4.

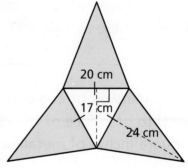

20 cm
17 cm
24 cm

_____

Find the surface area of each pyramid.

5.

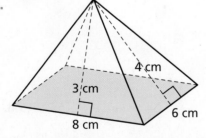

4 cm
3 cm
8 cm
6 cm

_____

6.

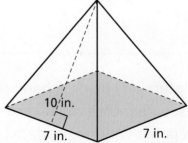

10 in.
7 in.
7 in.

_____

▶ Solve Real World Problems

Solve.

7. Marjorie bought this clock. How many square inches of glass did it take to make the clock?

_____

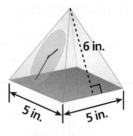

8. Lee bought a gift that came with this box. He wants to glue wrapping paper without any overlap to the 4 faces and base. How many square inches of wrapping paper will he need?

_____

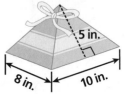

9. Nina is making containers to hold popcorn for a party. How many square inches of cardboard will it take to make 8 of these containers?

_____

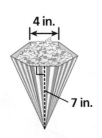

10. Tim made this paperweight in a crafts workshop. He glued metal to each face of the paperweight. How many square inches of metal did he use?

_____

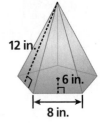

11. This bead is in the shape of a triangular pyramid. Each face of this bead has a surface area of about $\frac{1}{2}$ in.² How many square inches would it take to make a tight fitting cover for the bead ignoring any overlap?

_____

12. This ice sculpture will be on a banquet buffet table. How many square inches will it take to wrap the ice sculpture in paper with no overlaps?

_____

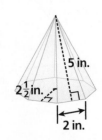

► Math and Packaging

Tiffany and her family grow berries and vegetables and sell them at a Farmers' Market. These are the berry baskets they use to package their berries.

1. Make a net for a berry basket with same dimensions as the one shown above on Quarter-Inch Grid Paper (TRB M19), cut it out, and use tape to form the berry basket.

▶ Make a Carry Container

Tiffany wants to make a carry container to hold three berry baskets so customers can carry them home without spilling or damaging the berries.

2. Tape two Quarter-Inch Grids (TRB M19) together so there are no gaps between grids. Draw a net for a carry container that will hold three berry baskets and take up the least surface area.

3. Use the net to find the surface area of the carry container.

_____

4. Cut out the net and form the carry container. Use the berry baskets you made to test that they fit in the carry container.

5. Tiffany's brother Aaron made a container fold down to make it easier to stack and carry them. He made a fold on each end of the front and back as shown below. Is this the best angle for folding? Use your carry container to try some different angles for folding and decide which one works best.

_____

_____

Focus on Mathematical Practices

▶ Vocabulary

Choose the best term from the box.

1. A _____ is a solid whose base can be any polygon and whose lateral faces are triangles. **(Lesson 4-4)**

2. A _____ is a solid figure that has two parallel congruent bases and rectangles for lateral faces. **(Lessons 4-1, 4-2)**

3. A(n) _____ is a line segment where two faces of a prism or pyramid meet. **(Lessons 4-1, 4-2, 4-4)**

▶ Concepts and Skills

4. Why is surface area measured in square units? **(Lesson 4-1)**

   _____

5. Why are the lateral faces of a right prism rectangles? **(Lesson 4-1, 4-2)**

   _____

   _____

6. Why are the lateral faces of a pyramid triangles? **(Lesson 4-4)**

   _____

7. How do you know how many rectangular faces a nonrectangular prism will have? **(Lesson 4-2)**

   _____

8. What is the minimum number of different surface areas of faces you need to find to calculate the surface area of a rectangular prism that is not a cube or a square prism? Explain. **(Lesson 4-1)**

   _____

   _____

Will the net form a solid figure? If not, fix the net. Then write the name of the solid figure the net will form. (Lessons 4-1, 4-2, 4-4)

9.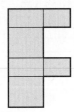

10.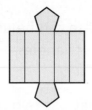

11.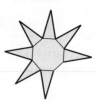

_____   _____   _____

Find the surface area. (Lessons 4-1, 4-2, 4-3, 4-5)

12.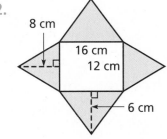
8 cm
16 cm
12 cm
6 cm

13.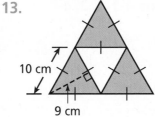
10 cm
9 cm

14.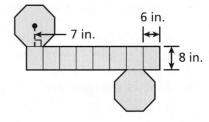
6 in.
7 in.
8 in.

_____   _____   _____

15.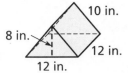
10 in.
8 in.
12 in.
12 in.

16.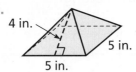
4 in.
5 in.
5 in.

17.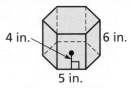
10 cm
15 cm
10 cm

18.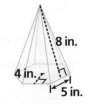
4 in.
6 in.
5 in.

_____   _____   _____   _____

▶ **Problem Solving**

Solve.

19. How much cardboard did it take to make this gift box. (Lesson 4-5)

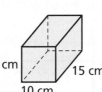
8 in.
4 in.
5 in.

_____

20. **Extended Response** How much fabric did it take to cover the table disregarding the overlap for seams? Describe a shortcut you can use to find the answer and explain why it works. (Lessons 4-1, 4-3)

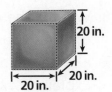
20 in.
20 in.
20 in.

_____

_____

_____

Reference Tables

Table of Measures

Metric	Customary

Length/Area/Volume

Metric

1 millimeter (mm) = 0.001 meter (m)

1 centimeter (cm) = 0.01 meter

1 decimeter (dm) = 0.1 meter

1 dekameter (dkm) = 10 meters

1 hectometer (hm) = 100 meters

1 kilometer (km) = 1,000 meters

1 hectare (ha) = 1,000 square meters (m^2)

1 square centimeter = 1 cm^2
A metric unit for measuring area. It is the area of a square that is one centimeter on each side.

1 cubic centimeter = 1 cm^3
A unit for measuring volume. It is the volume of a cube with each edge 1 centimeter long.

Customary

1 foot (ft) = 12 inches (in.)

1 yard (yd) = 36 inches

1 yard = 3 feet

1 mile (mi) = 5,280 feet

1 mile = 1,760 yards

1 acre = 4,840 square yards

1 acre = 43,560 square feet

1 acre = $\frac{1}{640}$ square mile

1 square inch = 1 in^2
A customary unit for measuring area. It is the area of a square that is one inch on each side.

1 cubic inch = 1 in^3
A unit for measuring volume. It is the volume of a cube with each edge 1 inch long.

Capacity

Metric

1 milliliter (mL) = 0.001 liter (L)

1 centiliter (cL) = 0.01 liter

1 deciliter (dL) = 0.1 liter

1 dekaliter (dkL) = 10 liters

1 hectoliter (hL) = 100 liters

1 kiloliter (kL) = 1,000 liters

Customary

1 teaspoon (tsp) = $\frac{1}{6}$ fluid ounce (fl oz)

1 tablespoon (tbsp) = $\frac{1}{2}$ fluid ounce

1 cup (c) = 8 fluid ounces

1 pint (pt) = 2 cups

1 quart (qt) = 2 pints

1 gallon (gal) = 4 quarts

Mass

1 milligram (mg) = 0.001 gram (g)

1 centigram (cg) = 0.01 gram

1 decigram (dg) = 0.1 gram

1 dekagram (dkg) = 10 grams

1 hectogram (hg) = 100 grams

1 kilogram (kg) = 1,000 grams

1 metric ton = 1,000 kilograms

Weight

1 pound (lb) = 16 ounces

1 ton (T) = 2,000 pounds

Volume/Capacity/Mass for Water

1 cubic centimeter (cm^3) = 1 milliliter = 1 gram

1,000 cubic centimeters = 1 liter = 1 kilogram

Reference Tables (continued)

Table of Units of Time
Time

1 minute (min) = 60 seconds (sec)	1 year = 365 days
1 hour (hr) = 60 minutes	1 leap year = 366 days
1 day = 24 hours	1 decade = 10 years
1 week (wk) = 7 days	1 century = 100 years
1 month, about 30 days	1 millennium - 1,000 years
1 year (yr) = 12 months (mo) or about 52 weeks	

Table of Formulas
Perimeter

Polygon P = sum of the lengths of the sides

Rectangle $P = 2(l + w)$ or $P = 2l + 2w$

Square $P = 4s$

Area

Parallelogram $A = bh$

Polygon $A = \frac{1}{2}n \cdot s \cdot h$ or $A = \frac{n}{2} \cdot s \cdot h$

Rectangle $A = lw$ or $A = bh$

Square $A = s^2$

Trapezoid $A = \frac{1}{2}h\,(b_1 + b_2)$

Triangle $A = \frac{1}{2}bh$

Surface Area of a Polygon

(informal) SA = sum of the areas of the faces

Volume of a Rectangular Prism

$V = lwh$ or $V = Bh$
(where B is the area of the base of the prism)

Distance Formula

$d = rt$

Properties of Operations

Associative Property of Addition

$(a + b) + c = a + (b + c)$ $\qquad$ $(2 + 5) + 3 = 2 + (5 + 3)$

Commutative Property of Addition

$a + b = b + a$ $\qquad$ $4 + 6 = 6 + 4$

Additive Identity Property of 0

$a + 0 = 0 + a = a$ $\qquad$ $3 + 0 = 0 + 3 = 3$

Additive Inverse

For every a there exists ^-a so that $a + (^-a) = (^-a) + a = 0$.
For $a = 5$, $5 + (^-5) = (^-5) + 5 = 0$

Associative Property of Multiplication

$(a \bullet b) \bullet c = a \bullet (b \bullet c)$ $\qquad$ $(3 \bullet 5) \bullet 7 = 3 \bullet (5 \bullet 7)$

Commutative Property of Multiplication

$a \bullet b = b \bullet a$ $\qquad$ $6 \bullet 3 = 3 \bullet 6$

Multiplicative Identity Property of 1

$a \bullet 1 = 1 \bullet a = a$ $\qquad$ $8 \bullet 1 = 1 \bullet 8 = 8$

Multiplicative Inverse

For every $a \neq 0$ there exists $\frac{1}{a}$ so that $a \bullet \frac{1}{a} = \frac{1}{a} \bullet a = 1$.
For $a = 5$, $5 \bullet \frac{1}{5} = \frac{1}{5} \bullet 5 = 1$.

Distributive Property of Multiplication over Addition

$a \bullet (b + c) = (a \bullet b) + (a \bullet c)$ $\qquad$ $2 \bullet (4 + 3) = (2 \bullet 4) + (2 \bullet 3)$

Properties of Equality

Reflexive Property of Equality	**Symmetric Property of Equality**
$a = a$	If $a = b$, then $b = a$.
Transitive Property of Equality	**Addition Property of Equality**
If $a = b$ and $b = c$, then $a = c$.	If $a = b$, then $a + c = b + c$.
Subtraction Property of Equality	**Multiplication Property of Equality**
If $a = b$, then $a - c = b - c$.	If $a = b$, then $a \bullet c = b \bullet c$.

Division Property of Equality

If $a = b$ and $c \neq 0$, then $a \div c = b \div c$.

Problem Types

	Result Unknown	Change Unknown	Start Unknown
Add to	Six children were playing tag in the yard. Three more children came to play. How many children are playing in the yard now? *Situation and Solution Equation:* $6 + 3 = c$	Six children were playing tag in the yard. Some more children came to play. Now there are 9 children in the yard. How many children came to play? *Situation Equation:* $6 + c = 9$ *Solution Equation:* $6 + c = 9$ or $9 - 6 = c$	Some children were playing tag in the yard. Three more children came to play. Now there are 9 children in the yard. How many children were in the yard at first? *Situation Equation:* $c + 3 = 9$ *Solution Equation:* $3 + c = 9$ or $9 - 3 = c$
Take from	Jake has 10 trading cards. He gave 3 to his brother. How many trading cards does he have left? *Situation and Solution Equation:* $10 - 3 = t$	Jake has 10 trading cards. He gave some to his brother. Now Jake has 7 trading cards left. How many cards did he give to his brother? *Situation Equation:* $10 - t = 7$ *Solution Equation:* $10 - 7 = t$ or $7 + t = 10$	Jake has some trading cards. He gave 3 to his brother. Now Jake has 7 trading cards left. How many cards did he start with? *Situation Equation:* $t - 3 = 7$ *Solution Equation:* $7 + 3 = t$

	Total Unknown	Addend Unknown	Both Addends Unknown
Put Together/ Take Apart	Ana put 9 dimes and 4 nickels in her pocket. How many coins did she put in her pocket? *Situation and Solution Equation:* $9 + 4 = c$	Ana put 13 coins in her pocket. Nine coins are dimes and the rest are nickels. How many are nickels? *Situation Equation:* $13 = 9 + n$ *Solution Equation:* $13 - 9 = n$ or $9 + n = 13$	Ana put 13 coins in her pocket. Some coins are dimes and some coins are nickels. How many coins are dimes and how many are nickels? *Situation Equation:* $13 = d + n$

	Difference Unknown	Bigger Unknown	Smaller Unknown
Compare[1]	Aki has 8 apples. Sofia has 14 apples. How many more apples does Sofia have than Aki? *Solution Equation:* $8 + a = 14$ or $14 - 8 = a$ Aki has 8 apples. Sofia has 14 apples. How many fewer apples does Aki have than Sofia? *Solution Equation:* $8 + a = 14$ or $14 - 8 = a$	**Leading Language** Aki has 8 apples. Sofia has 6 more apples than Aki. How many apples does Sofia have? *Solution Equation:* $8 + 6 = a$ **Misleading Language** Aki has 8 apples. Aki has 6 fewer apples than Sofia. How many apples does Sofia have? *Solution Equation:* $8 + 6 = a$	**Leading Language** Sofia has 14 apples. Aki has 6 fewer apples than Sofia. How many apples does Aki have? *Solution Equation:* $14 - 6 = a$ or $6 + a = 14$ **Misleading Language** Sofia has 14 apples. Sofia has 6 more apples than Aki. How many apples does Aki have? *Solution Equation:* $14 - 6 = a$ or $6 + a = 14$

[1]The comparing sentence can always be said in two ways: One uses more, and the other uses fewer. Misleading language suggests the wrong operation. For example, it says *Aki has 6 fewer apples than Sofia*, but you have to add 6 to Aki's 8 apples to get 14 apples.

	Unknown Product	Group Size Unknown	Number of Groups Unknown
Equal Groups	Seth has 5 bags with 2 apples in each bag. How many apples does Seth have in all? *Solution Equation:* $5 \cdot 2 = n$	Seth has 5 bags with the same number of apples in each bag. He has 10 apples in all. How many apples are in each bag? *Situation Equation:* $5 \cdot n = 10$ *Solution Equation:* $10 \div 5 = n$	Seth has some bags of apples. Each bag has 2 apples in it. He has 10 apples in all. How many bags of apples does Seth have? *Situation Equation:* $n \cdot 2 = 10$ *Solution Equation:* $10 \div 2 = n$

Problem Types (continued)

	Unknown Product	Unknown Factor	Unknown Factor
Arrays[2]	Jenna has 2 rows of stamps with 5 stamps in each row. How many stamps does Jenna have in all? *Solution Equation:* $2 \cdot 5 = s$	Jenna has 2 rows of stamps with the same number of stamps in each row. She has 10 stamps in all. How many stamps are in each row? *Situation Equation:* $2 \cdot s = 10$ *Solution Equation:* $10 \div 2 = s$	Jenna has a certain number of rows of stamps. There are 5 stamps in each row. She has 10 stamps in all. How many rows of stamps does Jenna have? *Situation Equation:* $r \cdot 5 = 10$ *Solution Equation:* $10 \div 5 = r$
Area	The floor of the kitchen is 2 meters by 5 meters. What is the area of the floor? *Solution Equation:* $2 \cdot 5 = a$	The floor of the kitchen is 2 meters long. The area of the floor is 10 square meters. How wide is the floor? *Situation Equation:* $2 \cdot s = 10$ *Solution Equation:* $10 \div 2 = s$	The width of the kitchen is 5 meters long. The area of the floor is 10 square meters. What is the length of the floor? *Situation Equation:* $r \cdot 5 = 10$ *Solution Equation:* $10 \div 5 = r$
Compare	Katie picked 5 times as many flowers as Benardo. Benardo picked 2 flowers. How many flowers did Katie pick? *Solution Equation:* $5 \cdot 2 = k$	Katie picked 5 times as many flowers as Benardo. Katie picked 10 flowers. How many flowers did Bernardo pick? *Situation Equation:* $5 \cdot b = 10$ *Solution Equation:* $10 \div 5 = b$	Katie picked 10 flowers. Bernardo picked 2 flowers. How many times as many flowers did Katie pick as Bernardo? *Situation Equation:* $m \cdot 2 = 10$ *Solution Equation:* $10 \div 2 = m$

[2]Array problems can also be stated using the number of rows and columns in the array: The apples in the grocery window are in 3 rows and 6 columns. How many apples are there?

Note: All of the division situations could also have the multiplication equation as the solution equation because you can solve division by finding the unknown factor.

Vocabulary Activities

▶ Word Review PAIRS

Work with a partner. Choose a word from a current unit or a review word from a previous unit. Use the word to complete one of the activities listed on the right. Then ask your partner if they have any edits to your work or questions about what you described. Repeat, having your partner choose a word.

Activities

▸ Give the meaning in word or gestures.

▸ Use the word in the sentence.

▸ Give another word that is related to the word in some way and explain the relationship.

▶ Crossword Puzzle PAIRS or INDIVIDUALS

Create a crossword puzzle similar to the example below. Use vocabulary words from the unit. You can add other related words, too. Challenge your partner to solve the puzzle.

Across

1. _____ and subtraction are inverse operations.

2. To put amounts together

3. When you trade 10 ones for 1 ten, you _____.

4. The answer to an addition problem

Down

1. In 24 + 65 = 89, 24 is an _____.

3. A combination of the digits 0, 1, 2, 3, 4, 5, 6, 7, 8, and 9.

4. The operation that you can use to find out how much more one number is than another.

Vocabulary Activities (continued)

▶ Word Wall `PAIRS or SMALL GROUPS`

With your teacher's permission, start a word wall in your classroom. As you work through each lesson, put the math vocabulary words on index cards and place them on the word wall. You can work with a partner or a small group choosing a word and giving the definition.

▶ Word Web `INDIVIDUALS`

Make a word web for a word or words you do not understand in a unit. Fill in the web with words or phrases that are related to the vocabulary word.

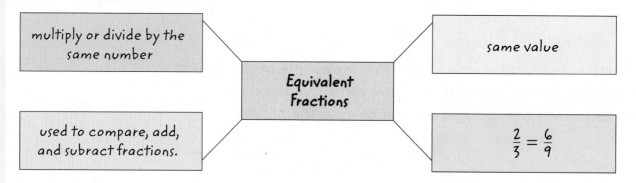

▶ Alphabet Challenge `PAIRS or INDIVIDUALS`

Take an alphabet challenge. Choose 3 letters from the alphabet. Think of three vocabulary words for each letter. Then write the definition or draw an example for each word.

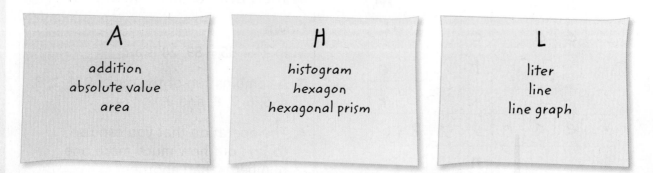

▶ Concentration PAIRS

Write the vocabulary words and related words from a unit on index cards. Write the definitions on a different set of index cards. Mix up both sets of cards. Then place the cards facedown on a table in an array, for example, 3 by 3 or 3 by 4. Take turns turning over two cards. If one card is a word and one card is a definition that matches the word, take the pair. Continue until each word has been matched with its definition.

area

the amount of surface covered or enclosed by a figure

▶ Math Journal INDIVIDUALS

As you learn new words, write them in your Math Journal. Write the definition of the word and include a sketch or an example. As you learn new information about the word, add notes to your definition.

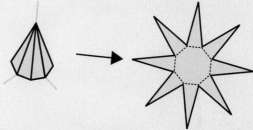

octagonal pyramid: Pyramid with a base that is an octagon and triangular faces that meet at a vertex.

Surface area: the total area of all the faces of a solid figure.

Vocabulary Activities (continued)

▶ What's the Word?   PAIRS

Work together to make a poster or bulletin board display of
the words in a unit. Write definitions on a set of index cards.
Mix up the cards. Work with a partner, choosing a definition
from the index cards. Have your partner point to the word
on the poster and name the matching math vocabulary word.
Switch roles and try the activity again.

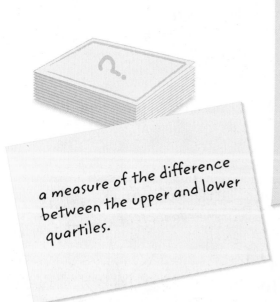

a measure of the difference between the upper and lower quartiles.

mean	median
box plot	dot plot
quartile	gap
first quartile	histogram
third quartile	range
cluster	outlier
mean absolute deviation	
interquartile range	

Glossary

A

absolute value A measure of the distance a number is from zero on a number line.

acute triangle A triangle with three acute angles. An acute angle has a measure that is greater than 0° and less than 90°.

Examples:

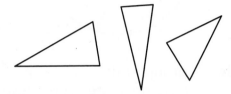

algebraic expression An expression that includes one or more variables.

Examples: $10(b + a)$
$7n$
$5x^2 - x$

area The amount of surface covered or enclosed by a figure. Area is measured by finding the number of same size units of area required to cover the shape without gaps or overlaps.

Associative Property of Addition The property that states that changing the grouping of addends does not change their sum. For any numbers a, b and c, $(a + b) + c = a + (b + c)$.

Example: $(7 + 8) + 2 = 7 + (8 + 2)$

Associative Property of Multiplication The property that states that changing the grouping of factors does not change their product. For any numbers a, b and c, $(a \cdot b) \cdot c = a \cdot (b \cdot c)$.

Example: $(9 \cdot 15) \cdot 20 = 9 \cdot (15 \cdot 20)$

B

bar graph A graph that uses the lengths of bars to show data. The bars may be horizontal or vertical.

Example:

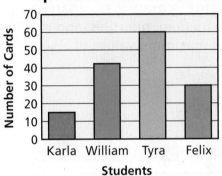

base of a figure For a triangle or parallelogram, a base is any side. For a trapezoid, a base is either of the parallel sides. For a prism, a base is one of the congruent parallel faces. For a pyramid, the base is the face that does not touch the vertex of the pyramid.

Examples:

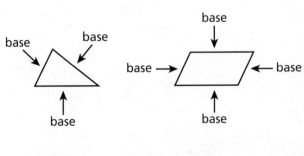

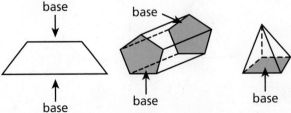

Glossary (Continued)

base of a number A number, variable, or expression that is raised to a power.

Examples: 4 is the base in the power 4^3. a is the base in the power a^7.

basic ratio A ratio in simplest form.

Examples: The basic ratio for $\frac{25}{30}$ is $\frac{5}{6}$.

The basic ratio for $\frac{12}{24}$ is $\frac{1}{2}$.

box plot A graphic summary that shows the median, quartiles, and minimum and maximum values of a set of data.

Example:

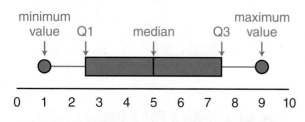

C

categorical data Data expressed as words that represent categories.

Example: Favorite sport: football, soccer, baseball, so on.

center of a polygon A point inside a regular polygon that is the same distance from each vertex.

Examples:

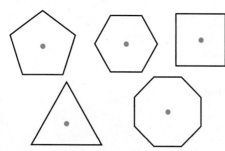

circle graph A graph used to display data that make up a whole. (Also called a *pie graph* or a *pie chart*.)

Example:

Sahil's Postcards from the U.S. by Region

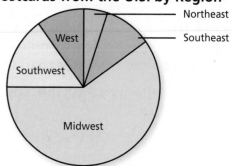

cluster A group of data values. A data set may have no clusters, one cluster, or more than one cluster.

Example:

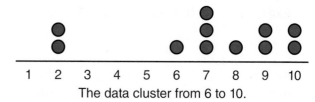

The data cluster from 6 to 10.

coefficient The number part of a term when the term is a number times a variable or a number times a product of variables.

Example: In $5x + 2xy$, 5 is the coefficient of the term $5x$ and 2 is the coefficient of the term $2xy$.

column In a data table, a vertical group of cells.

common denominator A common multiple of two or more denominators.

Example: 15 is a common denominator of $\frac{1}{3}$ and $\frac{2}{5}$.

$$\frac{1}{3} = \frac{5}{15} \qquad \frac{2}{5} = \frac{6}{15}$$

So, $\frac{1}{3} + \frac{2}{5} = \frac{5}{15} + \frac{6}{15} = \frac{11}{15}$

common factor A factor that two or more numbers share.

Example: 4 is a common factor of 12 and 20.

common multiple A number that is a multiple of two or more numbers.

Example: 24 is a common multiple of 8 and 6.

Commutative Property of Addition The property that states that changing the order of addends does not change their sum. For any numbers a and b, $a + b = b + a$.

Example: $18 + 21 = 21 + 18$

Commutative Property of Multiplication The property that states that changing the order of factors does not change their product. For any numbers a and b, $a \cdot b = b \cdot a$.

Example: $36 \cdot \frac{3}{4} = \frac{3}{4} \cdot 36$

compare ratios For two ratios, to state whether the amount of one quantity in a ratio is less than, greater than, or equal to the same quantity in the other ratio when the value of the other quantity in the ratios is the same.

complex figure A figure made by combining simple geometric figures, such as rectangles and triangles

Examples:

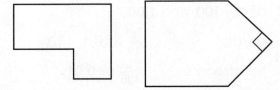

congruent Figures that are exactly the same size and shape.

Example: The bases of this pentagonal prism are congruent.

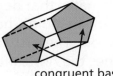

congruent bases

constant rate In a rate table in which the units are consecutive whole numbers, the constant difference in the values shown in the second column. Also the value in the second column when the number of units equals 1.

continuous data Data that represent an accumulation without interruption. Each data point is related to the data point before and after it.

Example: Temperature reading over a 24-hour period: 45°, 47°, 52°, and so on.

Glossary (Continued)

coordinate A number that determines the horizontal or vertical position of a point in the coordinate plane.

Example: The ordered pair (⁻7, 3) gives the coordinates that determine the position of the point shown on the graph below. The first coordinate, ⁻7, determines the horizontal position of the point. The second coordinate, 3, determines the vertical position of the point.

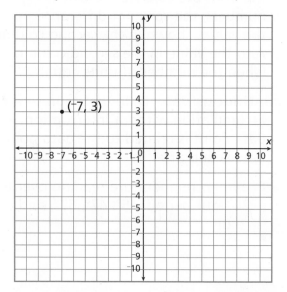

coordinate plane A plane together with a pair of perpendicular number lines that intersect at 0 on each number line. The perpendicular number lines are called axes.

Example: The coordinate plane is divided into four quadrants by the x- and y-axes. Below is the first quadrant of the coordinate plane.

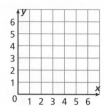

coordinates Each point in the coordinate plane corresponds to an ordered pair of numbers called its coordinates.

cross-multiplication A method used for solving proportions based on the fact that in a proportion, the cross-products are equal.

Example: $\frac{10}{15} = \frac{18}{27}$ is a proportion. The cross-products are equal.

$$\frac{10}{15} \times \frac{18}{27}$$

$$18 \cdot 15 = 10 \cdot 27$$

cube A rectangular prism with six congruent square faces.

cubic unit (unit³) A unit for measuring volume. It is the volume of a cube with each edge 1 unit long.

Example:

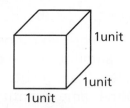

D

decimal A number with a decimal point in it. A decimal is another way to write a fraction. Some decimals are called decimal fractions because they represent fractions with denominators of 10, 100, and 1,000.

tenths	$\frac{1}{10}$ or 0.1
hundredths	$\frac{1}{100}$ or 0.01
thousandths	$\frac{1}{1,000}$ or 0.001

Example: The decimal 9.56 represents $9\frac{56}{100}$.

denominator The number below the bar in a fraction. It indicates the number of unit fractions made by dividing the whole into equal parts.

Example: In the fraction $\frac{3}{5}$, the denominator is 5.

$\frac{3}{5}$ ←——— denominator
It represents the 5 unit fractions (the 5 fifths) made by dividing the whole into 5 equal parts.

dependent variable In a relationship between two variables, the variable whose value depends on the value of the other variable.

Example: The cost of gas, c, depends on the number of gallons purchased, g. The cost, c, is the dependent variable.

diagonal A line segment connecting two vertices that are not next to each other.

Example:

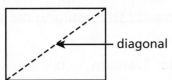

dimension The height, length, or width of a figure.

Examples: A line segment has only length, so it has one dimension.

A rectangle has length and width, so it has two dimensions.

A cube has length, width, and height, so it has three dimensions.

discrete data In a set of discrete data, each number is exact and the numbers are not related to each other.

Examples:

- The number of people who visit the library each day for a month.
- The number of books on each bookshelf at the library.
- The number of students in each grade in a school.

distance formula Distance (d) is the product of speed (r) and time (t).

Examples: distance = speed • time

or $d = rt$

Distributive Property Over Addition The property that allows us to distribute a factor to the terms of a sum or difference or to pull out a common factor from the terms of a sum or difference. For any numbers a, b, and c, $a(b + c) = ab + ac$.

Examples:
Distribute a factor:
$6(x - 2) = 6 \cdot x - 6 \cdot 2 = 6x - 12$
Pull out a factor:
$4y + 8 = 4 \cdot y + 4 \cdot 2 = 4(y + 2)$

dividend The number that is divided in a division problem.

Example:

$$56 \div 8 = 7 \qquad 8\overline{)56}^{\,7}$$

$56 \div 8 = 7$ — dividend

divisor The number that divides in a division problem.

Example:

$$56 \div 8 = 7 \qquad 8\overline{)56}^{\,7}$$

$56 \div 8 = 7$ — divisor

Glossary (Continued)

dot plot A display showing the frequency of numerical data. A dot plot uses a number line and dots to show how often the numbers in a set of numerical data occur.

Example:

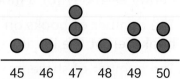

45 46 47 48 49 50

double number line A diagram with two number lines that shows how two quantities relate to each other.

Examples: The double number line below shows how distance and time are related for a person walking at a rate of 3 feet per second.

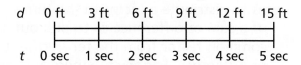

The double number line below shows what percent 0, 2, 4, and 6 millimeters are of 8 millimeters.

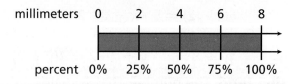

E

edge The line segment where two faces meet in a three-dimensional figure.

Examples:

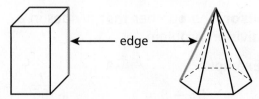

equation A statement that two or more expressions are equal. An equal sign (=) separates the two equal expressions in an equation.

Examples: $4 \cdot 2 = 8$

$x + 4 = 10$

equivalent expressions Expressions that always have the same value.

Example: $b + b + b$ and $3b$ are equivalent expressions.

equivalent fractions Fractions that represent the same number.

Example: $\frac{1}{2}$ and $\frac{3}{6}$ are equivalent fractions.

equivalent ratios Ratios that represent the same comparison. Equivalent ratios have the same basic ratio.

evaluate an algebraic expression Substitute values for the variables in an expression and then simplify the resulting numerical expression.

Example: Evaluate $10(b + a)$ when $b = 3$ and $a = 4$.
$10(b + a) = 10(3 + 4) = 10 \cdot 7 = 70$

exponent In a power, the small, raised number that indicates how many times the base is used as a factor.

Example: 3 is the exponent in the power 4^3.
$4^3 = 4 \cdot 4 \cdot 4 = 64$

expression A combination of one or more numbers, one or more variables, or both numbers and variables. An expression often includes one or more operations, but does not include an equals sign.

Examples: n

$$x - 9$$
$$5 \cdot 2^2$$
$$\frac{1}{2}\,bh$$

F

face A flat surface of a three-dimensional figure.

Examples:

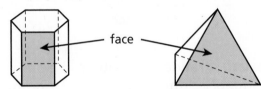

face

factor One of two or more numbers multiplied to make a product.

Example: $12 \cdot 4 = 48$

factor ⌐ ⌐ factor

factor of a number A number that divides evenly into the number.

Example: The factors of 18 are 1, 2, 3, 6, 9, and 18.

first quartile (Q1) The middle number, or mean of the two middle numbers, of the lower half of a set of data.

Example:

1 2 3 4 5 6 7 8 9 10 11 12

first quartile   median

So, Q1 = 3.5.

fraction A number that is the sum of unit fractions, each an equal part of a set or part of a whole.

Example:

$$\frac{3}{5} = \frac{1}{5} + \frac{1}{5} + \frac{1}{5} \text{ or } \frac{3}{5} = 3 \cdot \frac{1}{5}$$

G

gap An interval with no data. A set of data may have no gaps, one gap, or more than one gap.

Example:

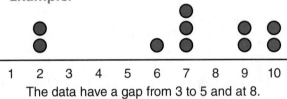

1 2 3 4 5 6 7 8 9 10
The data have a gap from 3 to 5 and at 8.

greatest common factor (GCF) The greatest factor that two or more numbers share.

Example: 15 is the GCF of 30 and 45.

H

height The height of a triangle or quadrilateral is the perpendicular distance from a base to a vertex that is not on the base. Finding this distance may require extending the base.

Examples:

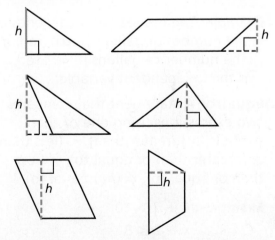

Glossary (Continued)

hexagon A polygon with six sides.

Examples:

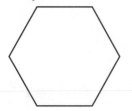

histogram A frequency display that uses bars to show the distribution of data in a set. Each bar represents an interval, or range, of data.

Example:

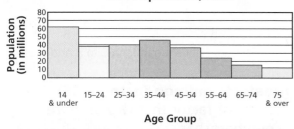

I

improper fraction A fraction in which the numerator is greater than or equal to the denominator.

Examples: $\frac{7}{5}$ $\frac{30}{8}$ $\frac{9}{9}$

independent variable In a relationship between two variables, the variable whose values influence the values of the other variable.

Example: The cost of gas, c, depends on the number of gallons purchased, g. The number of gallons purchased, g, is the independent variable.

inequality A statement that compares two expressions using one of these symbols: > (greater than), < (less than), ≥ (greater than or equal to), ≤ (less than or equal to), ≠ (not equal to).

Examples: $4 + 7 > 10$

$x - 2 \leq 8$

infinite Greater than any whole number; unlimited.

Example: $x > 3$ has an infinite number of solutions.

integers The set of integers includes whole numbers, their opposites, and zero.

interquartile range (IQR) A measure of the difference between the upper and lower quartiles. IQR is a way to describe the spread or variability of the data in a set.

Example:

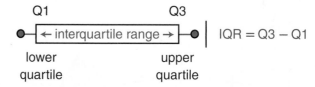

interval A range of numbers in a frequency display such as a histogram. An interval is sometimes called a *bin*.

inverse operations Operations that undo each other. Addition and subtraction are inverse operations. Multiplication and division are inverse operations.

Examples: $5 + 9 = 14$, so $14 - 9 = 5$.

$7 \cdot 9 = 63$, so $63 \div 9 = 7$.

L

lateral face A face that is not a base. Prisms have rectangular lateral faces and pyramids have triangular lateral faces.

Examples:

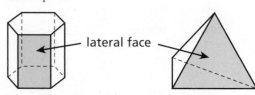

least common multiple (LCM) The least number that is a multiple of two or more numbers.

Example: 36 is the least common multiple of 9 and 12.

like terms Terms with the same variables raised to the same powers.

Example: In $6 + 2x + 1 + x$, 6 and 1 are like terms and $2x$ and x are like terms.

line graph A graph that uses a broken line to show changes in data.

Example:

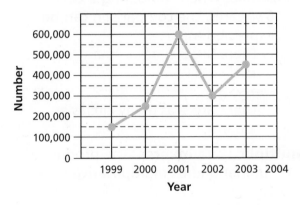

Deer Population in Midland Park

line of symmetry A line such that if a figure is folded on that line, the two parts will match exactly.

Example:

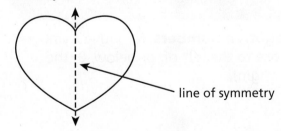

line of symmetry

line plot A diagram that shows the frequency of data on a number line.

Example:

```
                X
                X           X   X
        X   X   X   X   X   X
       ←─────────────────────────→
        45  46  47  48  49  50
```

linear equation An equation with a graph that is a line.

liquid volume A measure of how much a container can hold. Also called *capacity*.

M

mean A single number that summarizes all of the values in a set of numerical data. A mean is a measure of center that shows what the common data value would be if all of the data values were the same. A mean is calculated by adding the data values and dividing the sum by the number of values.

$\{8 \ \ 3 \ \ 1 \ \ 9 \ \ 14\}$ ← A set of numerical data.

$8 + 3 + 1 + 9 + 14 = 35$ ← Add.

$35 \div 5 = 7$ ← Divide. The mean of the data is 7.

Glossary (Continued)

mean absolute deviation A measure of variability that shows the average distance the data values in a set are from the mean.

Example:

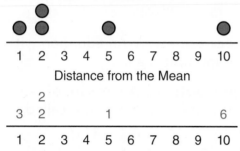

The Mean of These Values is 4

Distance from the Mean

The mean absolute deviation is $(3 + 2 + 2 + 1 + 6) \div 5 = 2.8$.

median A single number that summarizes the center of a set of numerical data. The median is the middle number, or the mean of the two middle numbers, when data have been arranged from least to greatest or from greatest to least. After the median has been calculated, one-half of the remaining numbers in the set will be less than the median and one-half will be greater.

Examples:

2 5 7 11 20   39 26 24 3
      ↑   ↑
 median = 7   median = 25

mixed number A number represented by a whole number and a fraction.

Example: $2\frac{1}{5}$ is a mixed number. It means $2 + \frac{1}{5}$.

mode The number or category that occurs most often in a set of data. A set of data may have no modes, one mode, or more than one mode. The mode is often used to describe categorical data.

multiple The product of a given number and a counting number.

Example: 3, 6, 9, 12, and so on are multiples of 3.

multiplicative comparison A way of comparing two quantities using *as many* or two amounts using *as much*. A multiplicative comparison can be expressed in two ways.

Example: When comparing 2 circles and 6 squares, the comparison can be expressed as:

There are 3 times as many squares as circles.

or

There are $\frac{1}{3}$ as many circles as squares.

multiplicative inverse The product of a number and its multiplicative inverse is 1.

Example: 6 is the multiplicative inverse of $\frac{1}{6}$.

$6 \cdot \frac{1}{6} = 1$ and $\frac{1}{6} \cdot 6 = 1$.

N

negative numbers Negative numbers are to the left of, or below, 0 (the origin).

net A two-dimensional flat pattern that can be folded into a three-dimensional figure.

Examples:

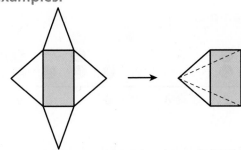

net of rectangular pyramid rectangular pyramid

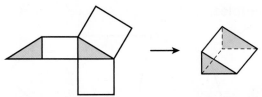

net of triangular prism triangular prism

number line A line that uses points to represent the distance and direction from zero of integers and other rational numbers.

Example:

-3 -2½ -2 -1½ -1 -½ 0 ½ 1 1½ 2 2½ 3

numerator The number above the bar in a fraction. It indicates the number of unit fractions the fraction represents.

Example: In the fraction $\frac{3}{5}$, the numerator is 3.

$\frac{3}{5}$ ◄— numerator

The numerator shows that the fraction represents 3 fifths: $\frac{3}{5} = \frac{1}{5} + \frac{1}{5} + \frac{1}{5}$.

numerical data Data involving numbers and quantities.

Examples:
- The number of students in each class in a school.
- The population of a city each year for the last ten years.

numerical expression An expression that does not include variables.

Examples: 36 − (2 + 9) • 3
20 − 8 ÷ 2

O

obtuse triangle A triangle with one obtuse angle. An obtuse angle has a measure that is greater than 90° and less than 180°.

Examples:

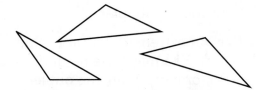

octagon A polygon with eight sides.

Examples:

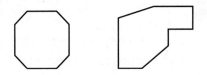

opposites Two numbers are opposites if they are the same distance from zero on a number line, but in opposite directions.

Examples: ⁻5 and 5
12 and ⁻12

ordered pair: Two numbers that are inside parentheses and have a comma in between them. Ordered pairs can represent points on the coordinate plane and are written as (x, y).

Examples: (5, 3) is an ordered pair, where x = 5 and y = 3.

Glossary (Continued)

Order of Operations A rule that states the order in which the operations in an expression should be done:
  1. Perform operations in parentheses.
  2. Simplify powers.
  3. Multiply and divide from left to right.
  4. Add and subtract from left to right.

origin The origin of a number line is the point at 0. The point of intersection of the *x*-axis and *y*-axis is called the origin of the coordinate plane.

outlier An extreme or distant value. A set of data may have no outliers, one outlier, or more than one outlier.

Example:

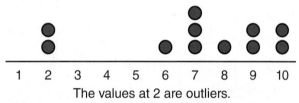

The values at 2 are outliers.

P
---

parallelogram A quadrilateral in which both pairs of opposite sides are parallel and opposite angles are congruent.

Examples:

peak The value (or values) that appear most often. A set of data may have no peaks, one peak, or more than one peak.

Example:

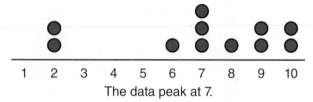

The data peak at 7.

pentagon A polygon with five sides.

Examples:

percent(%) An amount out of a hundred or per hundred.

Examples: $34\% = \frac{34}{100}$

$124\% = \frac{124}{100}$

perimeter The distance around a figure. It is the total number of same size units of length required to form the sides without gaps or overlaps.

perpendicular Lines, line segments, or rays are perpendicular if they form a right angle. A right angle has a measure that is equal to 90°.

Example:

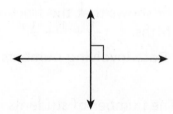

polygon A closed figure formed by line segments that do not cross each other.

positive numbers Positive numbers are to the right of, or above, 0 (the origin).

power An expression that includes an exponent and represents a repeated multiplication. The power of the expression is determined by the exponent.

Example: 4^3 (read "four raised to the third power") means $4 \cdot 4 \cdot 4$.

prism A solid figure with two congruent parallel bases.

Examples:

product The result of a multiplication.

Example: $12 \cdot 4 = 48$
└─────── product

proportion An equation stating that two ratios are equal.

pyramid A solid with a polygon for a base whose vertices are all joined to a single point.

Examples:

Q

quadrant The *x*- and *y*-axes divide the coordinate plane into four regions called *quadrants*. Beginning in the upper right quadrant and moving in a counterclockwise direction the quadrants are numbered using the Roman numerals I, II, III, and IV.

Example:

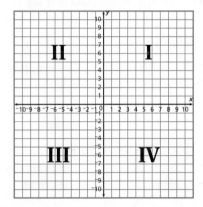

quadrilateral A polygon with four sides.

Examples:

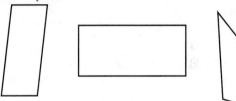

quartiles The values of the points that separate a set of data into four approximately equal parts.

quick drawing A sketch that summarizes a situation without showing unnecessary detail.

Example: Below is a quick drawing of the algebra-tile model for $3 + 2x$.

Glossary (Continued)

quotient The result of a division.

Example:

$$56 \div 8 = 7 \qquad 8\overline{)56}$$

with "quotient" labeling the 7 in each.

range A single number that summarizes the variability of the data in a set. The range is calculated by subtracting the least number in the set from the greatest.

Example: {5 2 16 10} ← The greatest value in this set is 16. The least value is 2.

$16 - 2 = 14$ ← Subtract. The range of the data is 14.

rate A special ratio in which the quantities may be described with different units (such as dollars and pounds).

rate table A two-column table showing the number of units in the first column and the value associated with each given number of units in the second column. When the units are listed as counting numbers in consecutive order, the values in the second column will show a constant difference; this constant difference is the unit rate.

Example: The rate table below shows how the unit days and the number of dollars saved are related. The constant difference is 3, and the unit rate is 3 dollars per day.

Number of Days	Dollars Saved
1	3
2	6
3	9
4	12

ratio Two quantities are in the ratio a to b if for every a units of the first quantity there are b units of the second quantity.

rational number Any number that can be expressed as a fraction $\frac{a}{b}$, where a and b are integers and $b \neq 0$.

ratio table A table showing equivalent ratios.

reciprocal The product of a number and its reciprocal is 1. The reciprocal of the fraction $\frac{a}{b}$ is $\frac{b}{a}$.

Example: $\frac{4}{3}$ is the reciprocal of $\frac{3}{4}$.

$$\frac{3}{4} \cdot \frac{4}{3} = 1 \text{ and } \frac{4}{3} \cdot \frac{3}{4} = 1$$

rectangular prism A solid figure with two rectangular bases that are congruent and parallel.

Example:

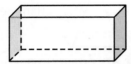

reflected point A given point and its reflected point are mirror images across the *x*-axis or *y*-axis of the coordinate plane.

Examples:

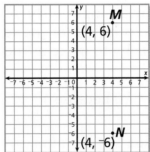

Point *N* is a reflection of point *M* across the *x*-axis.

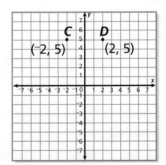

Point *C* is a reflection of point *D* across the *y*-axis.

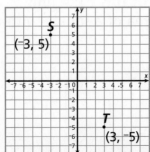

Point *T* is a reflection of point S across the *x*-axis and then the *y*-axis.

regular polygon A polygon with all sides the same length.

Examples:

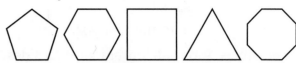

related parallelogram A parallelogram with the same base and height as its related rectangle or triangle.

Examples:

rectangle and related parallelogram

triangle and related parallelogram

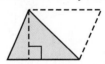

related rectangle A rectangle with the same base and height as its related parallelogram. A rectangle with the same base and height or half the height or base of its related triangle.

Examples:

parallelogram and related rectangle

triangles and related rectangles

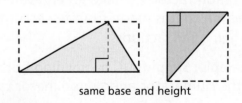

same base and height

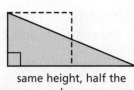

same base, half the height   same height, half the base

Glossary (Continued)

remainder The number left over after dividing a number that is not evenly divisible by the divisor.

Example: 32 ÷ 6 = 5 R2
The remainder is 2.

rhombus A parallelogram with all sides the same length.

Examples:

right triangle A triangle with one right angle. A right angle has a measure that is equal to 90°.

Examples:

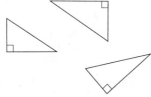

row In a data table, a horizontal group of cells.

S

scale of a model A ratio comparing the size of the model to the size of the actual object.

simplify a fraction Divide the numerator and denominator by a common factor to make an equivalent fraction that is made from fewer, but larger, unit fractions.

Example: Simplify $\frac{5}{10}$ by dividing both the numerator and denominator by 5.

$$\frac{5 \div 5}{10 \div 5} = \frac{1}{2}$$

simplify an expression Perform operations and combine all like terms.

Example: Simplify $3x + 5 + x + 2$.
$3x + 5 + x + 2 = 4x + 7$

slant height The height of a triangular face of a pyramid.

Example:

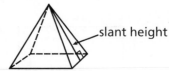
slant height

solution of an equation A number that can be substituted for the variable in an equation to make a true statement.

Example: $x = 4$ is a solution of $3x + 1 = 13$ because $3(4) + 1 = 13$ is true.

solution of an inequality A value that can be substituted for the variable in an inequality to make a true statement.

Example: $x = 10$ is a solution of $x + 3 < 20$ because $10 + 3 < 20$ is true.

solution set The set of all solutions of an inequality.

Examples:

This graph shows the solution set for $x > 3$.

This graph shows the solution set for $x \geq 3$.

square unit (unit²) A unit of area equal to the area of a square with one-unit sides.

Example:

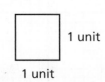
1 unit
1 unit

surface area The total area of all the faces of a solid figure.

symmetric data A data distribution that has a line of symmetry. The shape of the data on one side of the line of symmetry is the same as the shape of the data on the other side of the line.

Example:

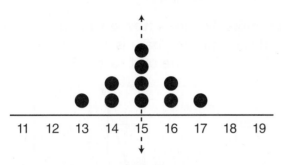

line of symmetry

T

tape diagram A drawing that looks like a segment of tape used to illustrate number relationships. Also known as a strip diagram, bar model, fraction strip, or length model.

Example:

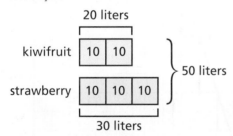

term Part of an expression that is added or subtracted.

Example: 4, $3b$, and b^2 are terms of the expression $4 + 3b + b^2$.

tessellation A pattern of closed figures that completely cover a surface with no gaps or overlaps.

Example:

third quartile (Q3) The middle number, or the mean of the two middle numbers, of the upper half of a set of data.

Example:

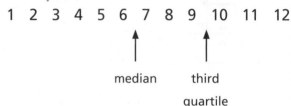

So, Q3 = 9.5.

trapezoid A quadrilateral with exactly one pair of parallel sides.

Examples:

U

unit cube A cube with one-unit edges.

unit fraction A fraction with 1 in the numerator.

unit length The distance between tick marks of a number line.

Example:

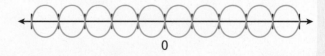

0

Glossary (Continued)

unit price The unit rate associated with a price or cost.

Example: 4 dollars per pound

unit rate The value associated with 1 unit.

Example: 5 miles *per* hour
3 dollars *every* week
2 apples *each* day

unit rate strategy A strategy in which a table is used to solve proportions.

Example: In this example, the unit rate, $\frac{3}{4}$ or $\frac{3}{4}$ to 1, is used to solve the proportion 3:4 = *x*:5.

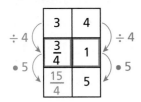

unit rate triangle When a rate situation is graphed in the coordinate plane, the unit rate triangle is a right triangle with base equal to 1 and height equal to the unit rate. The third side of the triangle is part of the line representing the rate situation.

Example: In the unit rate triangles in this graph, the base is 1 and the height is 3. The unit rate is 3.

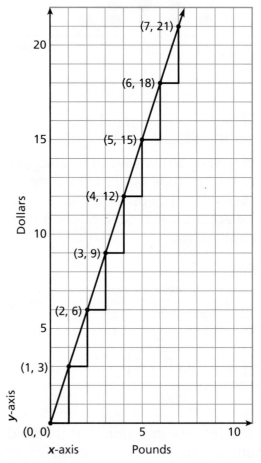

unsimplify Rewrite a fraction as an equivalent fraction with a greater numerator and denominator.

Example: Unsimplify $\frac{3}{5}$ by multiplying it by $\frac{6}{6}$.

$$\frac{3}{5} \cdot \frac{6}{6} = \frac{18}{30}$$

V

variable A letter or symbol used to represent an unknown number or a quantity that varies.

Example: $y = 2x$
  x and y are variables.

vertex A point common to two sides of an angle or polygon, or three edges of a solid figure. The point of a pyramid.

Examples:

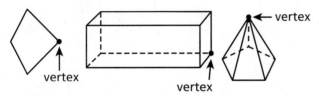

vertex   vertex   ← vertex

volume The amount of space occupied by a solid figure. Volume is measured in cubic units.

X

x-axis The horizontal number line in the coordinate plane.

x-coordinate The first number in an ordered (x, y) pair.

Y

y-axis The vertical number line in the coordinate plane.

y-coordinate The second number in an ordered (x, y) pair.